MLA GUIDE TO
Undergraduate
Research in Literature

MLA GUIDE TO

Undergraduate Research in Literature

Elizabeth Brookbank and
H. Faye Christenberry

Modern Language Association of America
New York   2019

To order MLA publications, visit mla.org/books. For wholesale and international orders, see mla.org/Bookstore-Orders.

The MLA office is located on the island known as Mannahatta (Manhattan) in Lenapehoking, the homeland of the Lenape people. The MLA pays respect to the original stewards of this land and to the diverse and vibrant Native communities that continue to thrive in New York City.

MLA Guides series

POD 2022 (second printing)

Library of Congress Cataloging-in-Publication Data
Names: Brookbank, Elizabeth, 1982- author. | Christenberry, H. Faye, 1963- author.
Title: MLA guide to undergraduate research in literature / Elizabeth Brookbank and
    H. Faye Christenberry.
Other titles: Undergraduate research in literature
Description: New York : Modern Language Association of America, 2019. Includes
    bibliographical references.
Identifiers: LCCN 2019011165 (print) | LCCN 2019015229 (ebook) | ISBN
    9781603294379 (EPUB) | ISBN 9781603294386 (Kindle) | ISBN 9781603294362
    (pbk. : alk. paper)
Subjects: LCSH: English literature—Research—Methodology—Handbooks, manuals,
    etc. | American literature—Research—Methodology—Handbooks, manuals, etc. |
    English literature—Electronic information resources—Handbooks, manuals, etc. |
    American literature—Electronic information resources—Handbooks, manuals, etc.
    | Internet research—Handbooks, manuals, etc. | Internet searching—Handbooks,
    manuals, etc. | Library orientation for college students—Handbooks, manuals, etc.
Classification: LCC PR56 (ebook) | LCC PR56 .B76 2019 (print) | DDC 820.72—dc23
LC record available at https://lccn.loc.gov/2019011165

Contents

Introduction

The purpose of this book is to offer guidance to undergraduate students working on research assignments for their English and American literature classes. While we hope it will also be helpful for college and university professors and instructors who teach literature to undergraduates, we are mostly concerned with you, the student. We describe key resources and offer tips on selecting the right databases for a research project, using these and other tools effectively to obtain various types of information, analyzing and evaluating the resources retrieved from searching, and managing and organizing your citations. Examples of assignment topics and tasks used in actual literature courses are given in each chapter to show you how research strategies can help you complete your course work successfully.

Students today are savvy about browsing the Web and locating resources on the Internet. Sometimes information on the Internet may be enough to support an argument or thesis statement for a research paper. But sometimes it will not be enough, or your professor may simply not accept what you find there. There are many tools available through the library that can help you locate the resources you need, or are required to use, for your assignment. Because they are often unfamiliar, however, and because there are so many out there—each focusing on different subjects and having different date ranges—it can be overwhelming to navigate and conquer the complex world of information on your own. That is why college and university librarians are here. Librarians are experts in information, in knowing what is available where and to whom and under what circumstances, in knowing what your professors and instructors expect of you and how you can meet those expectations.

In this book you'll learn how information is organized; what type of information you are expected to use in an academic context and how to recognize it; how to use the various tools available, from the library and on the Internet, to find resources; how to select the appropriate resource for the information you need; how to interpret what you discover through these tools; how to locate a physical book or journal on the library shelf or how to order it from another library; and how to manage your research so that you can create citations according to your teacher's requirements. In short, you'll learn how to be an academic researcher! We use examples to demonstrate things like the difference between scholarly and popular resources and how the right citation can strengthen an argument or thesis. You will be able to flip from one example, section, or chapter to another quickly and easily while you're working on your assignment. A glossary contains definitions and explanations of key terms used in the book; glossary terms appear in boldface at their first instance.

Because most research assignments for English and American literature courses require the application of scholarly secondary material—that is, material that describes or analyzes an author's work from an academic perspective—much of the book focuses on journal articles, book chapters, and so on. We also discuss book reviews, Web sites, encyclopedias, and other popular secondary sources and when it may be appropriate to use them. We discuss primary sources as well—what they are, how to locate them (both in print and online), and how to use them to support a thesis. We cover how to use the library database or catalog, subject-specific research databases, and the Internet to incorporate literary criticism, book reviews, primary sources, and contextual information into your research paper. This book also offers advice on thinking critically about information, establishing the authority of information and what type of source is appropriate to your paper, managing and citing bibliographies, and information on the more specialized resources you may need in upper-level literature courses or when writing a senior thesis.

There are too many resources available for students and scholars doing research in literature for us to cover them comprehensively. Instead, we give a selection of tools that are among the most important for undergraduates conducting research in English and American literature and other literatures written in the English language. If you are planning to major in English or are considering graduate school in English, you should be aware of these tools. Most of them are available in any research library and any larger public library. Check with your librarian if you need help finding one at your institution.

The research process is a fluid one and can sometimes be difficult to navigate. This guide, if used in conjunction with a research project, should help you understand

what types of information are available to you when you research an author or literary work

how and where to find specific primary and secondary resources needed to support a thesis statement

how to create a bibliography

what to do if you encounter roadblocks in your work

Your professors will notice an improvement in the quality of your work, and your grade will improve. What is more important, you'll acquire the skills and build the habits of mind that go with good research, and they will not only help you with future assignments but also empower you to think more critically about the world of information around you in your day-to-day life.

1

Starting the Research Process

In this book, we give you the key tools and strategies you need to successfully conduct academic literary research at the undergraduate level. Some of what you learn here will also be useful when you conduct research in other **academic disciplines**, but some is specific to literary research. Different disciplines—literature, history, biology, political science—have different expectations for their publications and research practices and different ways to measure the quality of their scholarship. If you are already familiar with conducting academic research in another discipline, therefore, you will find some things in this book that do not match what you know. But our advice will help you understand the expectations of your research assignments in literature courses. Although not everything in this book applies to every course you will take in college, there is considerable overlap among disciplines, so it will give you a good start. It will tell you what to look for and what questions to ask when you are faced with a research question or assignment in any field.

What happens before you begin what most people think of as research is in fact an important phase of the research process itself. The steps you take before you start plugging **keywords** into *Google* or into a library **database** can set you up either for success or frustration. It is our hope that this chapter will give you the tools and guidance you need to set yourself up for success. The first step is to make sure you understand what you are meant to do. Courses, professors, and assignments differ, but we are providing you with basic guidelines to help you understand your literary research assignment. We take you through the process of exploring a topic through preliminary research, then discuss the importance of keywords and the development of a search strategy.

Once you have a strategy, you are ready to begin searching for works that support, challenge, or enhance the interpretation or argument of your paper.

Even though that sounds like a straightforward and linear process, in practice good research is fairly messy, and it is **iterative**, which means that you will likely find yourself returning to some of the steps that you already took and that you will have increasingly detailed and complex questions to answer. This is a good thing: it is what is supposed to happen when one does research. For instance, you gather keywords as you go and may find that you should redo your initial searches with different keywords. Or there may be another aspect of the topic that interests you now, prompting you to change your thesis statement. Or you may find that the resources you identified in your search strategy are not fruitful, so you need to shift your focus to other resources.

Shifts in direction and going back to square one are perfectly normal and to be expected. You are not doing anything wrong. A good researcher is open to new information and to making changes, is flexible, and can adapt to meet an unforeseen challenge. This does not mean that you will never find yourself at a dead end, so we also address what to do if you get stuck. At the end of this chapter we describe five common research-related pitfalls and how to avoid them. Now let's get started— that research paper is due soon.

Understanding Your Research Paper Assignment

Literary research assignments vary widely, but there are some guiding questions that will help you understand what you are supposed to do. When in doubt as to the answer to any of these questions, check with your professor.

What Type of Assignment Is This?

If it is a research paper, you will be expected to use outside sources, not just your own ideas. There are various types of essay prompts and questions you may be asked to consider in your literature classes, but if you are being asked to write a research paper, you likely will be expected to **analyze** a work of literature and come up with an interpretation, judgment, or conclusion (Barnet and Cain 56; Durant and Fabb 10). Your interpretation must be supported with evidence from the text itself and from the outside sources you choose to use. You may or may not be asked to be **persuasive** in your essay—that is, to take a position on a certain topic or issue related to the work you are studying and get your reader to accept your interpretation, judgment, or conclusion. If you are asked to write a persuasive essay, the topic you choose should be **debatable**. If your topic is an obvious point that no one would debate, then there will be no need for argument in your paper.

What Types of Information Must I Use?

Be sure to note if there are specific sources you must use—class readings, for instance. Most undergraduate literature research assignments focus on analyzing or interpreting one or more **primary sources**. Primary sources in literature fall into two categories. The first is the creative work itself—the novels, poems, plays, and other kinds of artistic expression that you study and discuss in class. Examples are original creative works, such as *Pride and Prejudice*, by Jane Austen; fiction that is derived from the original, such as *Death Comes to Pemberley*, by P. D. James, which is based on *Pride and Prejudice*; and adaptations of the original for the stage or screen, such as the BBC's *Pride and Prejudice*, directed by Andrew Davies. The second category of primary sources is a work written or published in a time **contemporary** to the author's—for example, the author's diary or letters. Using primary sources in literary research is discussed more fully in chapter 6 of this book.

Your research assignment will likely ask you to use **secondary sources** to support your claims about the primary source at hand, regardless of whether those claims are made to inform, interpret, or convince. A secondary source is *about* the primary source: it discusses, analyzes, critiques, interprets, debates, or otherwise engages with it or with the materials contemporary to it. Examples of secondary sources are encyclopedia entries, blog posts, articles, and books. Most secondary sources that will be relevant to your literature courses are those that engage in **literary criticism**. That is, they are analyzing or interpreting a piece of literature, through close reading of the primary source and often with the support of other secondary sources, with the goal of illuminating, explaining, or recontextualizing some aspect of it.

When you review your assignment, look carefully at the require-ments for the secondary sources you should use. Are there specific sources that you are not allowed to consult? Many freely available Inter-net sources, such as blogs, personal Web sites, and online encyclopedias like *Wikipedia*, as well as many materials you may find at the library, such as print encyclopedias or book reviews, are generally off-limits, be-cause they do not engage in scholarly literary criticism. But there may be some research assignments in which you are allowed to use these more general, popular materials. It all depends on your professor and on your assignment and its requirements, which is why it is important that you understand what is being asked of you.

The secondary sources that you will use are most often **peer-reviewed**. Variously called *academic sources, scholarly sources, peer-reviewed sources, refereed sources, the literature,* and *scholarly literature*, these can be either books or articles, but it is important to understand that they are a specific kind of source and serve a specific purpose. They are not simply anything that is credible or that was written by an expert. A scholar could write a blog post or an article for a magazine that is a credible secondary source and meets the definition of *literary criticism*, but it is not a peer-reviewed source if it has not gone through the process of peer review before being published. In peer review, an article, book, or book chapter is examined by a group of other experts in the same aca-demic field. They evaluate its quality and the contribution that it makes to their field and say whether or not they think it should be published in the **scholarly journal or book**. What these scholars are looking for when making this determination is specific to their field; what makes a work publishable in literary criticism will differ from what makes it pub-lishable in sociology, philosophy, or physics. The peer review process is how scholars attempt to ensure that all the research and writing coming out of their field is of high quality and contributes to the body of human knowledge in that field, which is the goal of any **academic discipline**. This process is not infallible—it is still governed by human beings, after all—but it is rigorous.

Peer review serves the purpose of reporting on the research, interpretations, and theories of scholars in academia. It is a way for scholars to hold a conversation with one another about what they have discovered in their areas of expertise. Peer-reviewed works therefore often have a narrow focus. For example, published literature on the topic of *Jane Eyre* and marriage includes titles such as

"Metaphors and Marriage Plots: *Jane Eyre*, *The Egoist*, and Metaphoric Dialogue in the Victorian Novel," by Erik Gray

"Re-reading *Jane Eyre*: Not a Romantic Marriage Plot but a Tale of Evolving Feminist Consciousness," by Katie R. Peel

"Marriage in *Jane Eyre*: From Contract to Conversation," by James Phillips

Women's Search for Independence in Charlotte Brontë's Jane Eyre, by Claudia Durst Johnson

Books and articles like these are not the place to go if you want an overview of an author's work or the definition of a literary term or the pros and cons of a basic argument. These general topics are more likely to be covered in **reference sources** like those discussed in chapter 7. Your literature professor will want you to use peer-reviewed works to support the claims you make in your research papers not because they are the only good sources of information but because in college you must learn how to participate in the scholarly conversation, and that conversation is taking place in peer-reviewed books and articles.

In some academic disciplines, such as those in the natural sciences, most scholars publish their research in articles; in the humanities, books are more commonly published. Undergraduate researchers understandably gravitate toward articles, because who has time to read five books for a five-page paper? We encourage you not to discount books in your research, however: doing so will cause you to miss out on a lot of content relevant to your topic. Books are often easier to read than scholarly articles, partly because they tend to be directed to an audience beyond academics, partly because the author has more space in a book than in an essay to convey information and make points.

You do not need to read a book from cover to cover for your research assignment. Instead, read strategically. Look at the table of contents: the chapter titles will give you a sense of what the book is about. If only one chapter deals with your topic, read that chapter and not the rest. If the book has an **index**, this can enable you to home in on where your topic is discussed. If the book has no table of contents or index, read the introduction, where the author gives an overview of the book's contents.

How do you know that a book has been peer-reviewed? Some, even those written by scholars, have not been. If the publisher is a university press, the chances are good that the book is scholarly and peer-reviewed. But take a moment to investigate the publisher, look on the "About" page of its Web site for a mission statement or statement of **scope** (i.e., what types of things it publishes), and look for what its peer review policy is. If you are unable to find this information, ask a librarian for help. In general, if you are unsure about the acceptability of a source, ask your professor. We discuss in detail the evaluation of information sources—both those you find on the Internet and those you find using library tools—in chapter 4.

Are There Any Other Requirements I Should Know About?

Does your assignment say that there is a certain number of secondary sources you must cite in your paper? If you are limited in the number and want to ensure that you are picking the best sources, you will need to review and evaluate more than that number during your research.

There are other assignment requirements that you should be on the lookout for at the beginning. For example, will your professor assign points for the length of the paper, or for its tone, **citation style**, and **bibliography** (i.e., the sources you used)? Chapter 8 discusses citation styles and the tools you can use to manage your research.

Developing a Topic

There is a lot of good advice from other people—like the authors given in the works-cited list at the end of this chapter—about choosing and developing a topic for a research paper assignment. Much of this advice focuses on picking what interests you, what you are curious about, or what provokes a response in you, and on taking care that your topic is narrow enough so as not to overwhelm you (Durant and Fabb 17; Barnet and Cain 64).

The manageability of a topic involves not only its scope but also the resources available to you. Does your college library have books on the subject, or will you need access to an archive or some other special material that would mean a trip to another library? Your librarian can help you answer that question. Conducting a search in your library **discovery system** or **catalog**, discussed in chapter 2, or in the subject-specific databases available through your library, discussed in chapter 3, will give you a sense of what has been written about the primary work you are studying or the topic you are considering. You want a topic about which there has been enough published so that you can support your interpretation with outside sources. If entire books have been written about your topic, it may be too broad. The articles and book chapters that come up in your searches will give you an idea of the level of specificity you should aim for.

Background reading is also a good way to explore a potential topic. It can confirm whether or not the topic you are considering interests you. It can also show you if your topic is too broad and give you ideas for how to narrow it down. Reference materials, which are more general than peer-reviewed books and articles and contain entries that are usually short (e.g., encyclopedias, handbooks, and biographical dictionaries), provide easily digestible information quickly. They are discussed in chapter 7.

Another way to decide what to write about is to just go ahead and do some writing—in the form of brainstorming, freewriting, or journaling. These types of prewriting exercises, especially when paired with reading from your preliminary research, can help get your ideas flowing (Barnet and Cain 23–31). If you continue to be unsure about your topic—what it should include, how general or specific it should be—always ask your professor.

Keep in mind that this part of the research process is exploratory and low-stakes. You may decide after doing this preliminary searching, reading, and writing that your topic does not interest you after all—much better to realize that now, when you are still in the early stages of your work and have time to choose another topic! If you decide to stick with your topic, you are already on your way. If you read an encyclopedia entry or an article that interests you and is on-topic, check the end for a bibliography or a list of further readings. These are treasure troves for your research: lists of sources laid out for you that are related to your topic and were hand-picked by an expert. Stay flexible and open to how your topic may change, expand, or narrow depending on what your research turns up—during this and later phases of the process.

Developing a Search Strategy

Once you have a topic, take a little time to develop a search strategy before going further. This is a step that is easy to skip, because the next steps seem intuitive. But what happens if you cannot find what you are looking for where you thought you would find it? Or if you search for your topic and get no usable results? Or if you search for your topic and find a set of results that is much too large for you to review thoroughly? This is where having a search strategy comes in. A strategy makes your searching more focused and efficient, and it provides you with alternative plans when things do not go as you expect.

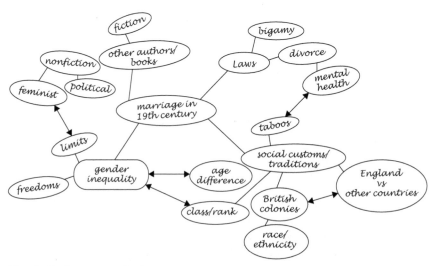

Fig. 1. Brainstorm mind map

First, think about what you want to learn about your topic. What questions would you have about it if you were the reader of your paper? What would you expect the author to cover? Make a list of subtopics that intrigue you; use a mind map or any other brainstorming technique (fig. 1). You will probably come up with more questions than you can cover in your paper, but that is a good thing. Remember, your research is part of the learning process. When you consider all the possible angles from which you could approach your topic and do research into a few of them, you should land on one or two that particularly interest you, and those should be the focus of your paper.

Possible research questions about marriage in *Jane Eyre*, by Charlotte Brontë

What were the laws surrounding marriage at the time *Jane Eyre* was written?

How would bigamy (or attempted bigamy) have been dealt with legally then? Would Rochester have faced any consequences?

What were the divorce laws? Was Rochester's portrayal of the difficulty of leaving Bertha, regardless of the state of her mental health, accurate for the time?

What were the social customs or traditions?

How would class, rank, wealth, and status have influenced what Rochester and Jane, from different socioeconomic classes, did?

Were the customs and beliefs around marriage different in the country versus the city? in England versus Europe? in England versus the United States?

What would the status and customs of someone living in the British colonies have been? What prejudices regarding race and ethnicity would have been involved?

Was age difference an issue, or was it the norm? Were there any taboos when it came to age in marriage (either young or old)?

How does the dialogue in the book about marriage either reinforce or diverge from these customs and traditions?

How were other authors at the time portraying marriage?

Was there any nonfiction writing about marriage then? If so, from what perspective? Was it political? feminist?

How were the genders treated differently, and how did this difference affect the general view of marriage?

What inequalities did women face in marriage? How were women limited in their behavior and life choices? How were men limited? What freedoms were granted to men and not women, and vice versa?

Did Jane's character and relationship with Rochester mirror what was common at the time? Or was it bucking the trend, making a feminist statement?

Next, think about where you might find the answers to your questions. What types of information and documents, in print or online, might serve the purpose? Consider the following types of sources and their uses.

Types of Sources

Reference sources (e.g., encyclopedias, dictionaries, handbooks, indexes, bibliographies)

WHAT: Usually provides an introductory overview to a topic, literary figure, or work. Often also includes a list of sources for further reading and research.

USE: These sources will get you started. They will give you background, context, and ideas for how to move forward in your research.

Popular sources (e.g., Web sites, blogs, social media, current newspapers, current magazines)

WHAT: Current news on a topic, opinions of a topic, figure, or work from pop culture or the media.

USE: These sources could be helpful if your topic is exploring the impact on pop culture of a certain work, or the portrayal of a certain work or figure in the media. Before you use them though, make sure your professor allows them.

Academic sources (e.g., peer-reviewed articles, scholarly books)

WHAT: Analysis, interpretation, and arguments made by experts in the field of literature about various topics, works, and literary figures.

USE: These are often the sources that your professors want you to use to support or challenge the points you are making in your analysis, interpretation, or argument. They will tell you what scholars in the field of literature have studied and theorized on when it comes to the work at hand.

Primary sources

WHAT: Primary sources (e.g., the work of literature itself, newspapers, magazines, and book reviews from the time the work was first published)

USE: In addition to textual evidence from the work at hand to support your claims and interpretation, you can use primary sources to give your argument or analysis valuable historical context.

What type of publication or Web site would have the information or document you're looking for? Ask yourself if there are different perspectives on any of these questions or subtopics that you should explore (fig. 2).

For the question about marriage law when *Jane Eyre* was written, consult historical legal codes, academic research, historical newspaper articles about trials and arrests, books about the history of the legal system in England, encyclopedias, and other reference sources (e.g., *Victorian Britain: An Encyclopedia*).

For the question about social customs or traditions of the time, consult history books, academic research, newspaper and magazine articles (e.g., magazines for ladies), etiquette manuals, encyclopedias, and other reference sources (e.g., *Victorian Britain: An Encyclopedia, Daily Life in Victorian England*).

For the question about how other authors at the time portrayed marriage, consult academic research, nineteenth-century fiction, history books, encyclopedias, and other reference sources (e.g., *The Encyclopedia of Victorian Literature, The Cambridge Companion to the Victorian Novel*).

For the question about how the genders were treated differently and how that difference affected the general view of marriage, consult history books, academic research, etiquette manuals, encyclopedias, and other reference sources (e.g., *Victorian Britain: An Encyclopedia, Daily Life in Victorian England*).

Using Keywords

Now that you have an idea of what you are looking for and what types of sources to use, how will you search for those sources? Your next step

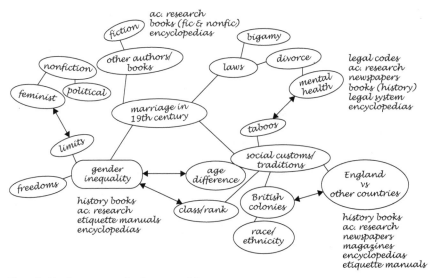

Fig. 2. Brainstorm mind map with source types

is to come up with a list of keywords. You probably have some keywords in mind immediately—the title of the book, the name of the author, and your topic, marriage. But the type of information you want should influence the words you use to look for it. If you are searching for scholarly literary criticism, it will be in texts that are written by and for an academic audience, so your searching will be more successful if you use the language of that field.

Brainstorm a little with this language need in mind—think of the words you have read in academic articles or have heard your professor use (fig. 3). For example, we usually don't use the word *matrimony* when we talk about marriage, but that synonym appears commonly in academic texts. Scholarly essays about marriage in *Jane Eyre* are often tagged in databases with the phrase *women's studies*, which is the academic discipline that studies gender issues. Even if you come up with only a few words at first, thinking intentionally about academic vocabulary will put you in the right mind-set. As your research progresses and you find scholarly sources that fit your topic, take note of the words they use—or the tags and subject headings, if you are working with a library database of the kind discussed in chapters 2 and 3—and add them to your keyword list.

Keep in mind that this starting point with your general topic may not be where you end up. Unless you are writing a senior thesis, you should not try to answer all the questions you brainstorm in step 1 of developing your research strategy. Go through the three-step process illustrated above several times as you decide which questions you are most interested in pursuing, and your questions will become more specific and complex. You will add questions, sources, and keywords as you narrow and deepen your research. Again, if you need help anywhere along the way, ask one of your librarians. Getting help at this early stage will save you time and stress when the deadline approaches.

Good research has its logic but is also an art. The strategy laid out here will serve you well in many situations, but there are always situations for which another strategy will be more successful. As you become more experienced with research and adept at developing and following a research strategy, you will learn how to customize this process to work for you.

marriage in nineteenth century	*gender issues*
matrimony	*women*
marital	*woman*
wedding	*male/female*
bigamy	*sex roles*
divorce	*sexism*
laws	*prejudice*
legal/illegal	*feminism*
social customs	*feminist*
culture	*women's studies*
traditions	*women's rights*
beliefs	*feminine*
taboos	*femininity*
religion	*inequality*
Victorian	*discrimination*
heterosexual	*justice*

Fig. 3. Keyword brainstorm example

The Research Process:
Five Common Pitfalls and How to Avoid Them

You now have the tools you need to start your research on the right foot, but even the most experienced researchers can make mistakes or run into obstacles. Here is a list of common research-related pitfalls and how to avoid them.

1. Deciding on the Right Answer
to Your Research Question before You Begin

Deciding on the conclusion you will draw in your research paper before you actually do the research and become aware of the scholarly conversation around your topic is a bad idea. Having the endpoint before you begin cuts off the possibility of your learning from your research. Remember that the entire point of scholarly literary criticism, which you are modeling with your paper, is to create new knowledge, not to report on what you already know. Your research may lead you to places you don't expect, may introduce you to ideas you did not know existed. You are beginning to participate in the scholarly conversation, and that participation entails having an open mind. You should listen to what others have to say on a subject before you draw your own conclusions and decide how you can add to what they have said. Starting your research by looking for books and articles that confirm what you have already decided is the right answer is not research. And what happens if there is no scholarly literature that fits your conclusion?

So by all means form your own ideas and theories and use them to guide the development of your research strategy, even guess at where you might end up, but keep an open mind throughout. You must be willing to see your topic from a new angle, willing to follow new information and go in directions you had not originally considered, willing to change your mind on the basis of what other scholars have written. Such flexibility will make your conclusion strong and well-informed.

2. Not Evaluating Your Sources
and, as a Result, Using Bad Information

Once a student, unfortunately unaware that *The Onion* is a satirical Web site, used an *Onion* article in an academic paper as evidence for her argument. This is a true story. You may know what *The Onion* is but cannot know about every single Web site that posts fake, biased, incorrect, or satirical information. Determining whether or not the sources you are considering are accurate and trustworthy is only the first step. You should also decide whether or not they are appropriate for your paper, whether or not they provide the best way for you to make your points.

For example, there are entries for nearly any topic in the online, crowdsourced encyclopedia *Wikipedia*, and chances are fair to good that the information you find there will be as accurate and trustworthy as that in other encyclopedias (Giles), but *Wikipedia* may not be the right source for you to use for a college-level research paper. Like any encyclopedia, it provides general, factual information on a variety of topics. But the secondary sources your professors want you to use to support the points you make in your research paper are generally those that analyze or interpret a work of literature with the goal of illuminating, explaining, or recontextualizing some element of it. As discussed earlier in this chapter, this is what literary scholars do and is the reason why your professors are most often looking for you to use scholarly articles or books as the outside sources for your research papers. Again, this is not to say that the information you get from *Wikipedia* is wrong. If you just needed to look up a definition of symbolism for a scintillating conversation with friends about your literature class (this is what students do with their free time, right?), *Wikipedia* would be a perfectly acceptable place to look—because the context and the type of information you need in that situation is different. In chapters 2 and 4, learn more about how to evaluate the sources of information that you plan to use in your literary research paper.

3. Being Afraid to Change Your Topic

There is no such thing as an objectively right or wrong topic. Because research tends to be a messy, iterative process, it is completely normal for you to feel unfocused or even confused in the beginning of it. We encourage you not to focus on picking the right topic but to think of this process as an investigation to figure out what you're really interested in and in that way to land on the topic that is right for you—and that fits the requirements of your paper.

You may find that the topic you first chose is not the right one for you—because it is too small (usually referred to by professors and librarians as "too narrow") or too big ("too broad") for your assignment, or maybe another topic seems more interesting to you now. Reluctance to change your topic is understandable: you have already put work into researching it and don't want to waste that time. But consider that time part of the learning process. Allow your topic to evolve as you do your research.

Consider, for example, that you are trying to write a five-page paper but discover that your topic has had whole books devoted to it—so you need to get more specific. The role of race in the writing of Langston Hughes is too big a subject for you, but you could perhaps write about how the speech of his African American characters is portrayed in a work or part of a work and compare it with how his white characters are represented (Barnet and Cain 299).

4. Not Keeping Track of Where You Got Your Information

You may feel that it takes too much time to create each citation as you go, but it takes much more time to sift through every source you looked at or to re-create your database and Internet searches looking for that quote you used on page 2. You don't need to use perfect MLA style for your citations as you go: just keep track of where you got your ideas and quotations during your research instead of leaving that task until the end.

You can keep track of your research by taking notes on what the source was, what idea it sparked for you, and how you plan to use it in your paper. Writing these types of notes or **annotations** for yourself will help you later if you need to go back and revisit a source or idea. Your system could be as simple as creating a list of links at the end of your draft that correspond to each citation in your paper. Or you could use one of the research organization tools that are available on the Internet or through your library—learn more about them in chapter 8.

5. Not Asking for Help

Librarians—this book was written by two of them—are there to help you. Wherever you are in the process of writing and researching your paper, whatever problems you are having, big or small, or even if you just want someone to bounce an idea off of, don't be shy, ask a librarian. You are new to academic research, so give yourself permission to get the help you need to succeed at it. There are different ways to reach out to the librarians at your college or university: you can approach them at the reference or information desk in the library, you can e-mail or call them to make a one-on-one appointment, or you can chat with them online through the library Web site. For this chat option, look on the library's site for something called "Chat with a Librarian," "Ask a Librarian," or "Ask Us."

Works Cited

Barnet, Sylvan, and William Cain. *A Short Guide to Writing about Literature*. Pearson Longman, 2006.

Durant, Alan, and Nigel Fabb. *How to Write Essays and Dissertations: A Guide for English Literature Students*. Routledge, 2005.

Giles, Jim. "Internet Encyclopedias Go Head to Head." *Nature*, 14 Dec. 2005, www.nature.com/articles/438900a.

2

Searching Your Library Discovery System or Catalog

In today's information landscape it seems that everything—all the information and resources we could ever want or need—is online. Not everything published online is available free to individuals, however. Much of it is proprietary, which means that you must pay to access it, and most scholarly material falls into this category. That is where your college or university library comes in. You will find many useful sources for your literary research in the online databases, books, and e-books that your library has purchased or pays to subscribe to. This includes subject-specific databases, which are discussed in the next chapter, as well as your library's database, where you can find scholarly and popular books (both physical and electronic), scholarly journal articles, **popular magazine** and newspaper articles, government documents, maps, movies, music, and anything else that your library physically owns or has electronic access to. These databases of library items, sometimes still called catalogs but increasingly called library discovery systems, are the subject of this chapter. We discuss the use of free Internet resources in the context of academic research in chapter 4.

To use a library discovery system effectively, you need to know the principles of database research. You will generally access your library's database of items through a search box or widget found on the campus library home page (figs. 4 and 5). Some libraries give their systems catchy names—the system at the University of Pennsylvania libraries is *Franklin*, the one at Carleton College's Gould Library is *Catalyst*—and sometimes the names are more straightforward, such as the University of Washington's *UW Libraries Search*. The system that your library uses may not look like the ones described in this chapter or have the same options, but most systems are structured in a similar way.

Is This like *Google*? Your Library's Discovery System

The short answer to the question of whether a library discovery system is like *Google* or any other search engine is both yes and no. Even though the search box of a discovery system may look just like that of any Internet search engine, it is different in some ways that will become important to you when you use it. Here are some tips for getting the most out of your library discovery system.

Search Using Relevant and Precise Keywords

A library discovery system is designed to be searched through keywords that match information in the database, as is done by an Internet search engine. But the discovery system does not have access to the full text for

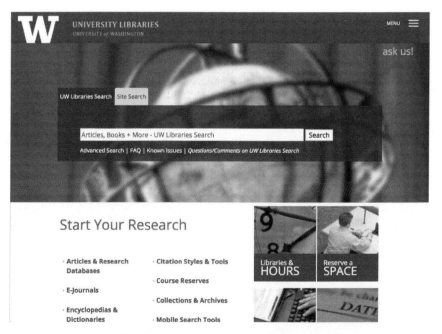

Fig. 4. Home page for the University of Washington libraries

many of the items it contains—especially books—the way that *Google* has access to the full text of the Web pages and documents it searches. Therefore the keywords you use to search a discovery system are usually being matched with more general, metalevel information, such as title, author, table of contents, and the back cover description of a book in the database. Use words that are likely to show up in those places, as opposed to words that might simply be discussed somewhere in the text.

The library discovery system is also not as intuitive as *Google*: it generally searches for exactly what you type in the search field, not what you meant to search. So when you search a discovery system, make sure you spell everything correctly and leave out common words, such as *the*, *what*, *is*, *if*, and *an*. Do not enter an entire sentence or question in the search box. *Google* may give you a good result when you type in "What imagery is used in 'The Lady of Shalott'?," but your library discovery system will probably not, because it will search for the sentence as a whole and not assume that you want all the results that use any of the most relevant words in that sentence.

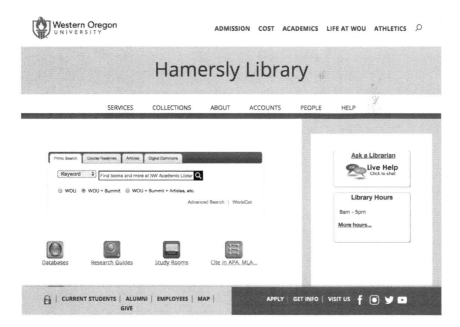

Fig. 5. Home page for the Western Oregon University library

When you search a discovery system, enter only the most relevant and uncommon words in your research question or topic. In the example above, those would be *imagery* and *"Lady of Shalott"*—notice we put the whole title in quotation marks (including the "of," because it is part of the title). Enclosing the full title in quotation marks tells the database that you want to find items that have that full, exact phrase, not those that have only one or two of the words in the phrase. Searching these two keywords or terms together in your library database should give you many usable results.

As discussed and demonstrated in chapter 1, it is a good idea to take the time to brainstorm a list of keywords that scholars are likely to use when discussing your topic. The payoff is that you will be more successful in your searching and find content that you cannot find on the Internet. The items in a discovery system tend to be weighted toward

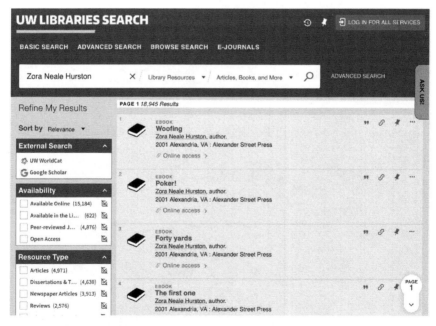

Fig. 6. Searching for *Zora Neale Hurston* at *UW Libraries*

scholarly books and research articles, the types of information sources that are generally more appropriate to your context, which is academia.

Get to Know Your Library Discovery System Interface

Most libraries allow you to begin your search from the library home page using an embedded search box. Usually there will be a simple box for you to type your keywords and click Search. Let's say that you want to search for books by the author Zora Neale Hurston. Putting her name in the main *UW Libraries Search* (fig. 6) results in nearly nineteen thousand items: print books, e-books, images, DVDs, scholarly articles, newspaper articles, book reviews, and more.

One advantage of a library discovery system is that it allows you to find many different types of materials from various databases and sometimes even from other libraries. The system acts as a clearinghouse for books in your library, books from other libraries if you are part of

PRINT BOOK
Zora Neale Hurston
Harold Bloom;
©2008 New York : Bloom's Literary Criticism

📖 Available at UW Tacoma Library Stacks (PS3515.U789 Z96 2008) and other locations >

ASK US!

Send to

✉ E-MAIL   „ CITATION   🔗 PERMALINK   🖨 PRINT   >

Get It

Fig. 7. Learning more about Harold Bloom's *Zora Neale Hurston*

a **consortium** that shares materials, articles from more specific databases, and more.

In the main portion of the screen is a list of the results of your search. For each item you are given the citation information—title, author, publisher, journal title if applicable, year published—and the information you need to locate it in your library, and whether or not it is available to be checked out. The buttons or links that are part of this result will look different depending on your discovery system. You may have to click on the title of the work to learn more about it (fig. 7), or there may be a "More Info" link (fig. 8). The details provided may include the table of contents, a description of the book from the publisher, the length of the book, as well as the **Library of Congress subject headings** (LCSH) that have been assigned to a book. The Library of Congress is the research library for Congress and the unofficial national library of the United States, which creates and maintains a central list of subject headings for all books published in this country so that they can be searched

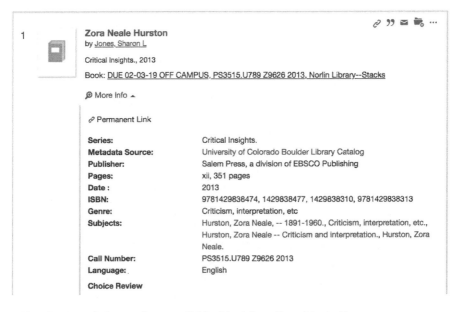

Fig. 8. More information on *Critical Insights: Zora Neale Hurston*

and accessed in all libraries (more on LCSH in the next section). If the item is an e-book, journal article, or other online resource, there will be a button or link directing you to the item with some tag like "Online Access," "Full Text Online," or "View Online."

Use the Database Options to Narrow or Expand Your Results

Although having access to all these different materials from different places can be helpful, it can also be overwhelming. Just as you would not attempt to look at all the millions of pages of results from a *Google* search, no one expects you to review all the results you generate from a general search through a library discovery system that results in eighteen thousand items. Once you are presented with an initial set of results, you have options that allow you to home in on what you need instead of sifting through page after page of results.

These options are generally available in a side bar—as in the *UW Libraries Search* under "Refine My Results" (fig. 6). They are known by various names, including **facets** and **limiters**, but whatever they are called, they will make your set of results smaller and more specific. The options in the *UW Libraries Search* are representative of the types of options you will encounter in most library discovery systems:

Resource type—print books, e-books, articles, dissertations. Since you are looking for books by Zora Neale Hurston, you can select "print books" or "e-books" to narrow your results.

Publication date

Physical location, either in a library or on a campus (this option varies from library to library)

Language

Author-Creator. Since you are looking for books *by* Hurston, you can select her name here to ensure that all your results are books she wrote as opposed to books *about* her.

Library of Congress classification or subject terms—the official tags used by the library to categorize the subject of each item in your results. If you are looking for books *about* Hurston (biographies, literary criticism of her work, etc.), you can select her name here to limit your results in that way.

These options are usually dynamic: the limiters displayed will change depending on your set of results. For example, if results from a given search contain no print books, the option to limit to print books will not appear.

The Library's Special Language: Library of Congress Subject Headings

Librarians use Library of Congress subject headings to describe and categorize the content of each book so that the book is searchable in various systems, databases, and library catalogs (fig. 9). The headings that librarians can choose from are therefore limited to those that have been approved by the Library of Congress. The benefit of this system is that the headings are universal to all kinds of systems and libraries. If you are

LC subject headings:
The Lady of Shalott in the Victorian Novel by Jennifer Gribble

Tennyson, Alfred Tennyson, Baron, 1809-1892. Lady of Shalott
Tennyson, Alfred Tennyson, Baron, 1809-1892 -- Influence
English fiction -- 19th century -- History and criticism
Arthurian romances -- Adaptations
Women and literature -- England -- History -- 19th century
Medievalism -- England -- History -- 19th century
Social isolation in literature
Romanticism -- Great Britain
Middle Ages in literature
Solitude in literature
Women in literature

Fig. 9. Example of Library of Congress subject headings

searching for literary criticism of the work of a certain author, you can search that author's name and the LCSH "Criticism and Interpretation" to find the books you want in any library database in the country. Usually the subject headings are links in the system, so that you only have to click on them to get a new set of results of all the books, e-books, and articles in the system that are tagged accordingly. The LCSH system is not perfect; it has the problems inherent in any effort to pin down the English language, because there are different ways to describe the same concept and because the living language is always changing. Therefore the word choices and phrasing of the LCSH are not always the most natural or commonly used, and are sometimes even antiquated or controversial in the light of social progress in many areas of society today. Think of the LCSH almost as a different language for you to learn, the language of a database, and use the headings to add to your keyword list in ways that improve your search in your library's discovery system.

Moving beyond the Basics

Using the Advanced Search Form

If you know exactly what you are looking for and want to skip the process of narrowing down a large set of results, most library databases let you use an advanced search form, which is basically several search boxes that allow you to choose various options all at once before you begin your search. Most advanced forms look like the examples shown in figures 10 and 11: several rows of search fields, each row having several menus with various options. In the example form in figure 10, the first menu you encounter is a drop-down list of searchable **fields** in the database. In the second menu, you apply a search method to the field you chose. Then comes the empty box for you to supply the word or words you wish to search. Before these options repeat in the next rows, there is a drop-down menu of the connector words (also called **Boolean operators**) that are meant to join multiple search terms in ways that change how the database searches for them. The second set of options is generally, as in figures 10 and 11, various menus or checklists and includes such fields as publication date, material type, language, and start and end date for your search. Many advanced search forms will also have a field for the scope of your search:

> your own library—physical and online materials your college or university library has access to
>
> your library and other libraries—plus physical materials in other libraries
>
> your library, other libraries, and other databases—plus online materials from any other source your library can search, including subject-specific databases and Web pages

Searching for Specific Types of Information

If you are doing research for books of literary criticism about *Frankenstein*, by Mary Shelley, you can type the word *Frankenstein* into the first search field, select the "Subject" option from the first drop-down menu, and select "Contains" from the second drop-down menu. This results in books about *Frankenstein*—that is, they have the word *Frankenstein* in

---

Search for: ⦿ Library Resources   ◯ Course Reserves

Show Only: Articles, Books, and More ▼

Any field ▼ contains ▼

Material Type
All items   ▼

AND ▼ Any field ▼ contains ▼

Publication Date
Any year   ▼

+ ADD A NEW LINE

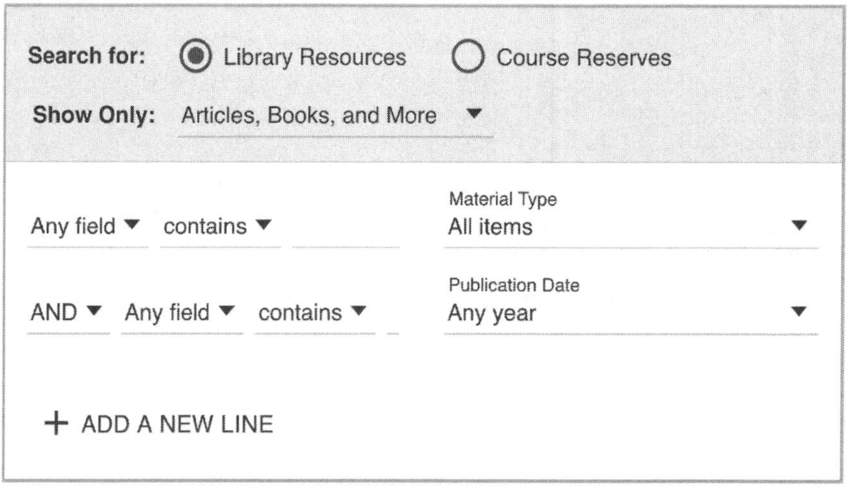

Fig. 10. Advanced search form at *UW Libraries*

one of their assigned Library of Congress subject headings. This set of results is not limited to literary criticism, however, and you will find many
books about film and theater adaptations of *Frankenstein*.

Using Boolean Operators

To make your results more precise, you can add keywords like *literary
criticism*, *criticism*, or *interpretation* to the second row of your search or
in any field available. To make sure that your new search turns up books
that have *Frankenstein* and *literary criticism* as subject terms, you will
need to think about how your new keywords relate to your existing keywords and make that relation clear to the database by using Boolean operators. The reason you added keywords is that the first results you got
from searching *Frankenstein* included books that were irrelevant. You
want only books that contain in their database records both the word
Frankenstein and the phrase *"literary criticism"* (keep the quotation marks
when entering the phrase to ensure that it is searched as a phrase). You
instruct the database to do this by choosing AND from the menu of con-
nectors between the first and second rows. This Boolean operator limits

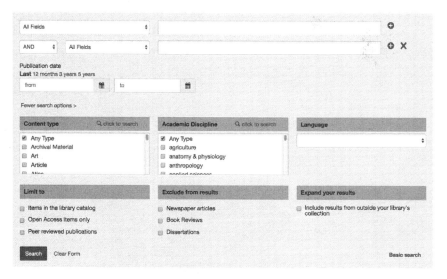

Fig. 11. Advanced search form at the University of Colorado library

your results to books that contain all the keywords you ask for. Other connector words have different functions. OR broadens your results to include books that contain either your first keyword or your second, or your third, and so on. OR is useful when you would like to get all the results in the database for synonyms or similar phrases. For instance, you could search for *Frankenstein* AND *criticism* OR *interpretation* to get all books about *Frankenstein* that contain either *criticism* or *interpretation* as keywords. The third and last Boolean operator is NOT. It excludes a word or phrase from your results. It is useful to keep irrelevant results out of your search. See figure 12 for a visual illustration of the different effects of Boolean operators.

Limiting by Date, Format, Language, and So On

To make your search more precise using the advanced search form, you can select some or all of the fields in the second set of options on the form. The example forms in figures 10 and 11 provide two ways for you to limit your search to a date range. In the "Publication Date" menu, you can consider books published only in the last two, five, ten, and so forth years. Alternatively, you can specify a day, month, and year range for your search—for example, everything published between 1 January 1818, the year *Frankenstein* was first published, to 1 February 1851, when Mary Shelley died. You can also limit your results to the type of material (books, e-books, articles, audiovisual sources), a specific language, or a search scope, which designates where you are searching.

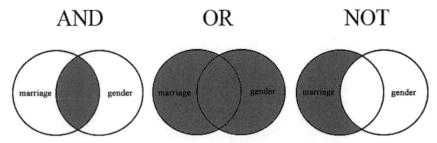

Fig. 12. Diagrams for the three Boolean operators

You do not have to use the advanced search form to take advantage of most of these options. In most cases you can do a standard search and limit your results by using the facets presented to you on the results screen. The advanced search form in a discovery system is simply a shortcut for this process. If your library still uses a traditional catalog search system, you will have more need for the advanced search form. An advanced searching technique that can be useful in either a discovery system or a traditional catalog is the use of special characters. The most popular special character is the asterisk, which allows you to search the system using **truncation**, in which the asterisk stands in for any combination of letters after it. For example, searching for *child** would return results like "child," "children," "childhood," and "childish." You will find that some discovery systems automatically assume that when you search for *child*, you want all these other forms as well. For the ones that don't, however, knowing how to use truncation is beneficial.

In using truncation it is important to choose the right point at which to place the asterisk—if there are too few initial letters or if the word is short, you will end up with too many results. Truncation can be helpful when you want results that contain either the American or British spelling for a word—searching *theat** to get both "theater" and "theatre," for example. Using truncation in this way to find results for words like "color" and "colour," however, will not work as well, because a search for *colo** will result in too many irrelevant words. But don't be afraid to try it. Experimenting, learning from both your successes and your failures, is a good way to get familiar with searching these systems.

Using Discovery System Personalization

Most discovery systems allow you a set of personalized options, so that you can save your searches and their results. Once you sign into the Western Oregon University or University of Washington system, for example, you have access to what it calls "My Favorites" (fig. 13), where you can save your results, come back to them later, and pick up where you left off. Your system's personal account options will probably be called something different and look different, but the ability to organize them in your account will likely exist in some form. If you cannot find this option or have trouble using it, ask one of your librarians.

Using Traditional Library Catalogs

Some libraries still use a traditional catalog system instead of a discovery system. If your library is one of these, the catalog will give you results only from that library, and these results will not include articles available online through any databases your library subscribes to—you will need to search the databases separately, as described in chapter 3. Many of the tips, tools, and strategies for searching that have been explained in this chapter, however, will still apply. Your options will be fewer; you will likely need to search by title, author, or subject heading and will not have all the facets or limiters that we discussed earlier. To broaden and narrow your search, you will need more general or specific keywords, need to add criteria, or need to use special characters. Most traditional catalogs offer search tips—look for a "Help" tab or on the page with the advanced search form.

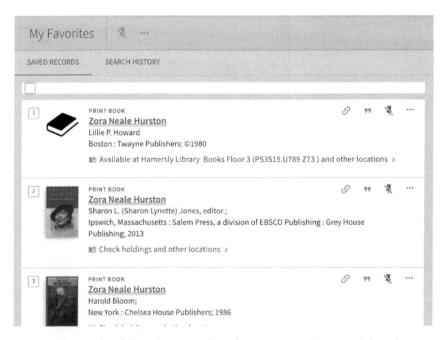

Fig. 13. Example of "My Favorites" at the Western Oregon University library

Using Materials from Other Libraries

Your search results in a discovery system may include books and articles from other libraries, but whether or not you see them depends on the search scope you choose, an option that is present in most systems. Your ability to take advantage of materials from other libraries will depend on your college or university library. Some do not allow undergraduates to order books from other libraries, or they do but ask that a fee be paid for the service. Most make this option available for free, however, so it is worth investigating. The general name for accessing books from other libraries is **interlibrary loan**. *WorldCat* is a large database that indexes over two billion items from over ten thousand libraries worldwide so that they can share with one another. You can search *WorldCat* on the Web (fig. 14), but most libraries have a personalized link to it that signs you in as a patron of that library with the ability to request books. Look for a link to search *WorldCat* on your library's Web site.

Some libraries in the same geographic area have created partnerships with agreements in place that make it easier and faster for them to trade materials than it is through the *WorldCat* system. Examples of these geographically based groups are the Orbis-Cascade Alliance in the Pacific Northwest, the Washington Research Library Consortium, and OhioLINK. If there are other universities in your area, you should be able to use their materials as a visitor. If your library belongs to a regional consortium, there will likely be an option in the discovery system to request a book or scholarly article from other libraries in that consortium. In the University of Washington and Western Oregon University systems, this option appears under the heading "Get It" in the item record (fig. 15). In other catalogs, you may have to click on the title of the item and then look in the detailed record for a button or link that says something along the lines of "Request This Item." Since this service is usually available only to people affiliated with a college or university, you will probably need to sign in to your discovery system to see this option.

When you request an item from other libraries—either through traditional interlibrary loan in *WorldCat* or through a somewhat faster consortium agreement—be aware that it will take time for you to receive it. It could take up to two weeks for a book to be shipped from one library to another. If you are ordering an article, chances are that it will be transmitted online, but this process could still take several days. Talk to your librarian about the specific policies and time frames for interlibrary loan at your library. But do not be shy about requesting these materials: libraries provide these services to help you in your research.

Choosing the Right Library Sources for Your Assignment

When you conduct research for an academic assignment, using your library's discovery system can be more efficient and precise than attempt-

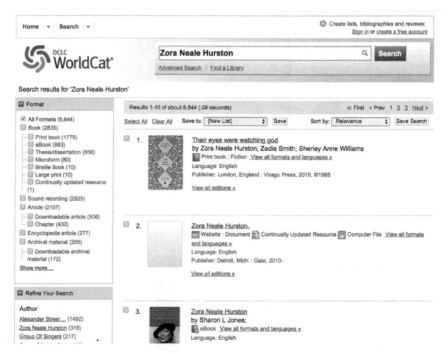

Fig. 14. Searching for *Zora Neale Hurston* in *WorldCat*

ing to find reliable academic sources on the Internet, because the library systems were created for searching scholarly information. This does not mean, however, that the books and articles in a library system are always reliable: there are no silver bullets when it comes to research. A library offers tools to make your research easier and better, but you must still employ your critical thinking skills when it comes to evaluating a source and deciding whether or not to use it for your assignment.

Because library discovery systems contain a plethora of information—not just books but also articles of all kinds, government documents, e-books, and even Internet sites—there are bound to be some sources that are not appropriate for an academic context. It is a common misconception that just because a source comes from the library, it must be reliable.

Additionally, reliability and credibility are not the only criteria for you to decide whether a source is the right one for your assignment. Evaluating a source of information means more than simply deciding

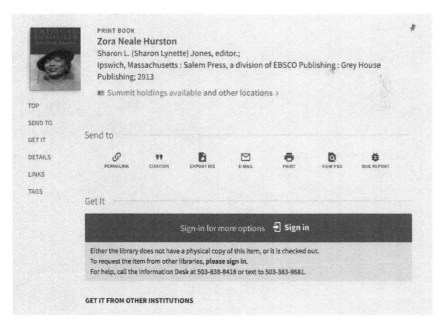

Fig. 15. Example of a "Get It" page

whether or not to trust what it is saying. Truth is certainly an important consideration, but evaluation also involves deciding whether or not a source is the right one for your purpose. Even a peer-reviewed scholarly article may not always be the best fit. If your assignment is a traditional research paper and your professor requires you to support your argument with three peer-reviewed sources, you will obviously need to limit your research to focus solely on peer-reviewed academic articles and books. The ideal way to achieve this is to make use of your library discovery system. You can also limit your search results in a subject-specific database of the type discussed in the next chapter. If you use *Google Scholar* or some other Internet search engine, however, you will need to look for clues to make sure that your sources are scholarly and peer-reviewed, as discussed in chapter 4. But if your assignment is to analyze how an author's work is treated in contemporary popular culture, you will probably not be required to limit your sources of information to scholarly ones and can use pop culture magazines and Web sites. There is no "one size fits all" approach to research—context matters. The type of information source that your professor will accept as appropriate will depend on the class and the assignment.

3

Searching
Subject-Specific Databases

When you learn how to search a library catalog using advanced techniques, you will know how to navigate other databases that your library provides. It may be necessary to look beyond your library catalog, because no one tool covers every publication on a particular discipline, author, or literary work. You have a great number of options, but we focus here on the most important resources available in the field of literary research. In this chapter we look at a few databases and answer the following questions: What types of materials do they cover? When should one be used and not another? We also review some of the search techniques you learned in chapter 2 and add to them.

A research database is basically a large collection of data that have been organized so that users can easily search and retrieve information in different ways. The library databases discussed in chapter 2 are very large and general and include materials from all subjects in all formats (books, articles, DVDs, maps, etc.). But most databases available through the library focus on a specific subject area. These are excellent tools to be aware of, because they have search features that are designed for the discipline they target. For example, researchers in many areas of the sciences rely on conference proceedings or technical reports to supplement their work. Databases in engineering or computer science will cover such proceedings and reports. Scholarship in most of the humanities disciplines relies on books, book chapters, journal articles, and doctoral dissertations. Search features designed for scholars rather than general readers are added to databases to improve discoverability of issues and themes of interest to researchers of literature—for instance, an author is designated by nationality, a literary work by genre. In this chapter we look at *Literature Resource Center* and the *MLA International Bibliography*.

You may also need to investigate interdisciplinary tools like EBSCO's *Academic Search, JSTOR*, and *Project MUSE*. Because these databases cover many different subject areas, they are a good place to start looking for information. The drawback is that the depth of coverage on any single subject is limited. Also, they will not provide special search features that help you identify issues or themes in literary studies.

How to Select the Right Database

Before you select a database for your research project, consider the parameters of your assignment, then check with your librarian for advice. There are three key questions to keep in mind: Do you need peer-reviewed sources? Is your topic interdisciplinary in focus? Is your author or literary work new?

Do You Need Peer-Reviewed Sources?

Does a source need to be an in-depth analysis of a work—a scholarly journal article, book, or book chapter—to meet the criteria of your project? Or should it be more timely, like a news magazine article reporting on a recent event? Or some combination of the two? Databases often contain both scholarly, peer-reviewed books and journals and sources such as newspapers and popular magazines, and some tools will provide a means of limiting your search results to one or the other. If the database you select does not have such options, you must be prepared to figure out how best to limit results on your own.

What Is a Peer-Reviewed Source?

In the peer review process, a journal article, book, or book chapter is read and analyzed by experts in the field. These experts (often called external readers or simply reviewers) comment on the subject matter, the quality of the writing, the strength of the argument presented, and whether or not the work adds to the scholarly conversation in that academic field. If the readers do not agree that the author has presented a successful paper, it will not be published unless revised to meet critical standards. The criteria will vary according to the field. Peer review takes place for selected **periodical** and book content, depending on the publishers. Articles in *Time* or *Newsweek* rarely have such strict vetting before publication, but those popular magazines serve a different purpose in the world of information. Most of the content in them and on news Web sites is provided to inform or entertain a general audience rather than to present scholarly findings and theories.

Some library databases, like the *MLA International Bibliography* and *Academic Search*, can tell you if a periodical resource has been peer-reviewed: all you need to do is check a box or limit your search accordingly. This is not an option for book chapters, but most academic presses peer-review their books before publication. If you need to determine if a book has been peer-reviewed, a good place to start is to look at the publisher's Web site for author submission guidelines.

How to Determine If a Book or Article Has Been Peer-Reviewed

When you scroll through a text in a database, the following criteria can give you clues as to whether or not it has been peer-reviewed:

- The author is a scholar or professional practitioner. The author's **credentials** should be readily available, either at the beginning of the article or in the back of the journal or book.
- Glance at the pages: ten or more should have text without glossy illustrations or advertisements.
- The content will be an in-depth analysis or extensive overview of a topic.
- The intended audience will be scholars, not a general reader.
- There is typically a bibliography at the end, showing that the author did research in the field.

In chapter 4, you will find more discussion about evaluating sources—both peer-reviewed and not—for credibility, authenticity, and appropriateness.

Is Your Topic Interdisciplinary in Focus?

If your topic is interdisciplinary, you will need to search more databases. For example, if you are researching marriage and gender equality in Jane Austen's *Pride and Prejudice*, you will find plenty of literary criticism on the novel and gender themes in a database like the *MLA International Bibliography*, because its primary focus is literature. But if you wish to investigate the history of marriage in eighteenth-century England to get a better understanding of the issues in Austen's novel, you will need to search a database that is devoted to cultural and social history, like *Historical Abstracts*, or an interdisciplinary database, like *JSTOR* or *Project MUSE*. For more information on these three databases, see the **appendix** to this book.

Is Your Author or Literary Work New?

Authors who have been studied for many years can be challenging to research because of the large amount of scholarship that has been published about them. If studying Shakespeare, for example, you will need to focus your search strategies carefully to avoid having to sift through too much information. On the other hand, because it takes time for authors to become noticed by scholars and because peer-reviewed articles take time to be published, you may not find any literary criticism on a new work of literary fiction—for example, C. E. Morgan's *The Sport of Kings*, which was nominated for the 2017 Women's Prize for Fiction. When this book was being written, there were no articles in the *MLA International Bibliography* on the novel and only three items on C. E. Morgan—two of which were author interviews. If you want to write a research paper on Morgan or her work, you must broaden your search (to the theme of Appalachian life, for instance, since she lives in and writes about Kentucky) or you can look for book reviews to gain insight on how a new author is being received. Book reviews become available quicker than literary criticism, but they are also limited, being brief and providing summaries more than analysis. We discuss book reviews and how to find them in chapter 5.

Subject-Specific Databases

Literature Resource Center is a good starting point for finding articles on your topic and is available in most academic and large public libraries. The database covers literary criticism, book reviews, and biographical sketches on writers around the world and in all time periods. A nice feature is that it automatically breaks down search results into categories that are easily identifiable. For instance, if you are doing research on Margaret Atwood's *The Handmaid's Tale*, you can do a basic search and see results listed in the following groups: literary criticism, biographical articles, topic overviews, book and film reviews, and multimedia resources (fig. 16). If you are interested only in criticism, you can click

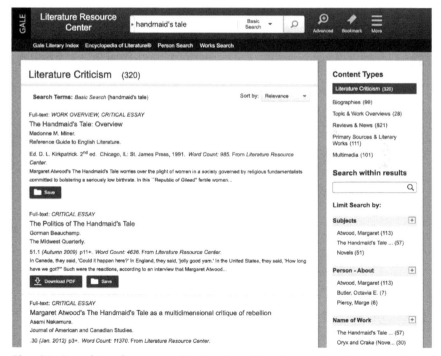

Fig. 16. Searching for Atwood's *Handmaid's Tale* in Gale's *Literature Resource Center*

on that link and go directly to those results. Most of the articles in *Literature Resource Center* are available in full text, so there is no need to determine if your library has the publication in its physical collection. Using the "Advanced Search" option, you can limit your search to peer-reviewed journals only (fig. 17). Advanced search screens, when they are available, are the best way to look for information, because they allow you to focus on such things as type of resource, publication date range, language, or audience.

The *MLA International Bibliography* is the most comprehensive resource for students and scholars conducting research in the field of modern languages and literatures, including English and American literatures. Currently, the bibliography covers content from more than 4,400 periodicals dating back as far as 1881 and includes book chapters and monographs from over a thousand publishers. Because it also indexes doctoral dissertations and scholarly Web sites, you will not find another database that compares with the *MLA International Bibliography* for locating scholarship on an author, literary work, or theme in literature.

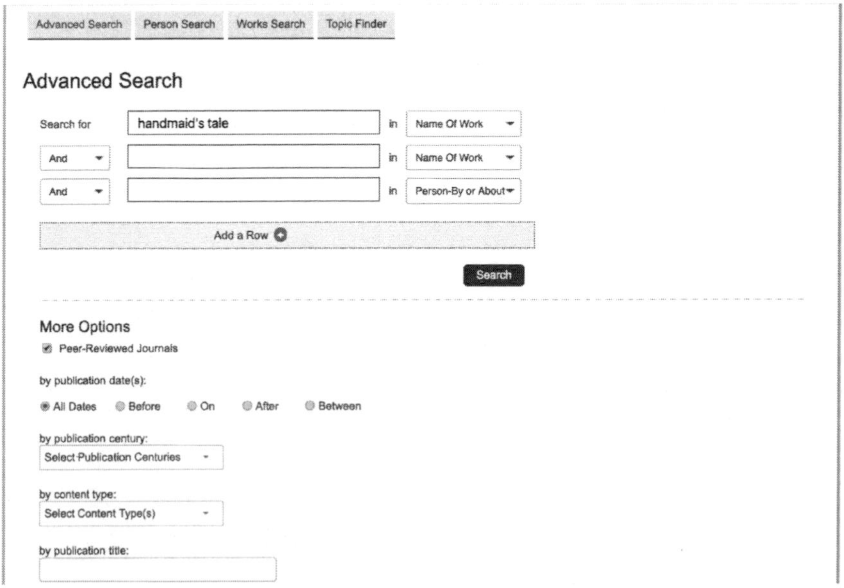

Fig. 17. Limiting the search to peer-reviewed journals

For a brief video on the history of the bibliography and a list of useful tutorials on using it, see the Modern Language Association's Web site (www.mla.org/bibtutorials).

To illustrate the advantage of searching the MLA bibliography, let's look again at *The Handmaid's Tale*. We found 56 critical essays on it in *Literature Resource Center*; the MLA bibliography has 208. Searching the bibliography is similar to searching any database—you can do a simple keyword search and use Boolean operators (AND, OR, NOT) and truncation (*) to focus your searches (explained in chapter 2). Add the phrase "Film Adaptation" in the next box, and you will retrieve only criticism of the film version of *The Handmaid's Tale*. More detailed tips on advanced searching are examined below.

There are three important pieces of advice to consider when using the MLA bibliography.

1. On the focus or approach of the text. The database has few abstracts, so look closely at the title of the essay or book chapter and the subject headings used to describe the work. Subject headings are assigned to every entry and will appear in the full record (see chapter 2 for a refresher on what subject headings are). You can see what subject headings are used in the bibliography by going to the thesaurus. Figure 18 is a screenshot of the full record of Celia Florén's "A Reading of Margaret Atwood's Dystopia, *The Handmaid's Tale*." The subject headings assigned to this article indicate that the author is discussing the themes of women and dystopia in *The Handmaid's Tale*. "Feminist approach" means that Florén uses feminist literary theory to examine the novel.

2. On access to full-text resources. The bibliography has selected full-text resources, so you may need to check your library's catalog to make sure you can get the essays or books you have identified for your project. Most libraries have a link in each database record that takes you directly to the library discovery system or catalog to check for full text. If you have trouble determining if something is available at your library, ask your librarian.

3. On the language of the content. The bibliography, which is international, contains non-English-language resources. If you want to limit your results to one language, like English, or to exclude one or more languages, you can use the "Language" option under "Refine Results."

Searching: **MLA International Bibliography** | Choose Databases

a reading of the handmaid's tale	Select a Field (optional) ▾	**Search**
AND ▾	Select a Field (optional) ▾	Clear ⑦
AND ▾	Select a Field (optional) ▾	⊕ ⊖

Basic Search   Advanced Search   Search History

‹ Result List   Refine Search   ‹ **3 of 5** ›

A Reading of Margaret Atwood's Dystopia, The Handmaid's Tale

Authors:	Florén, Celia
Source:	pp. 253-64 IN: Cornut-Gentille D'Arcy, Chantal (ed. and foreword); García Landa, José Angel (ed. and introd.); Gender, I-Deology: Essays on Theory, Fiction and Film. Amsterdam, Netherlands; Rodopi; 1996. (465 pp.)
ISBN:	9789051839692; (hbk.); 9789051839586; (pbk.)
Series:	Postmodern Studies: 16
General Subject Areas:	*Subject Literature:* Canadian literature *Period:* 1900-1999 *Primary Subject Author:* Atwood, Margaret (1939-) *Primary Subject Work:* The **Handmaid's Tale** (1985) *Classification:* novel
Subject Terms:	treatment of dystopia; women; feminist approach
Document Information:	*Publication Type:* Book Article *Language of Publication:* English *Update Code:* 199701 *Sequence Numbers:* 1997-1-7095
Accession Number:	1997028127

Fig. 18. Full record at the *MLA International Bibliography* of Florén's essay

Advanced Searching in the *MLA International Bibliography*

The "Advanced Search" screen illustrates just how sophisticated the search options are in the MLA bibliography. For instance, you can look for a particular publication type (book, journal article, dissertation), retrieve scholarly, peer-reviewed journals only, focus on what was published within a specific date range, or limit your search to English language content (fig. 19). Look to the right of the search box and click on the down arrow, and you will see a list of searchable fields that narrow your search. Each field of a **bibliographic record** contains a piece of information that describes the content—the type of resource, the date the work was published, a brief description of what the work is about. If you are researching Atwood's works in the context of how they fit (or do not fit) in the genre of science fiction, you can search the bibliography to find articles published exclusively in the journal *Science Fiction Studies* by typing the name of the journal in the search box and selecting "SO Journal Title" in the drop-down box (fig. 20). Another example is the field "Literary Theme," which refers to anything a literary work is about, focuses on, or uses as a motif. If you search for *dystopia* as a keyword in

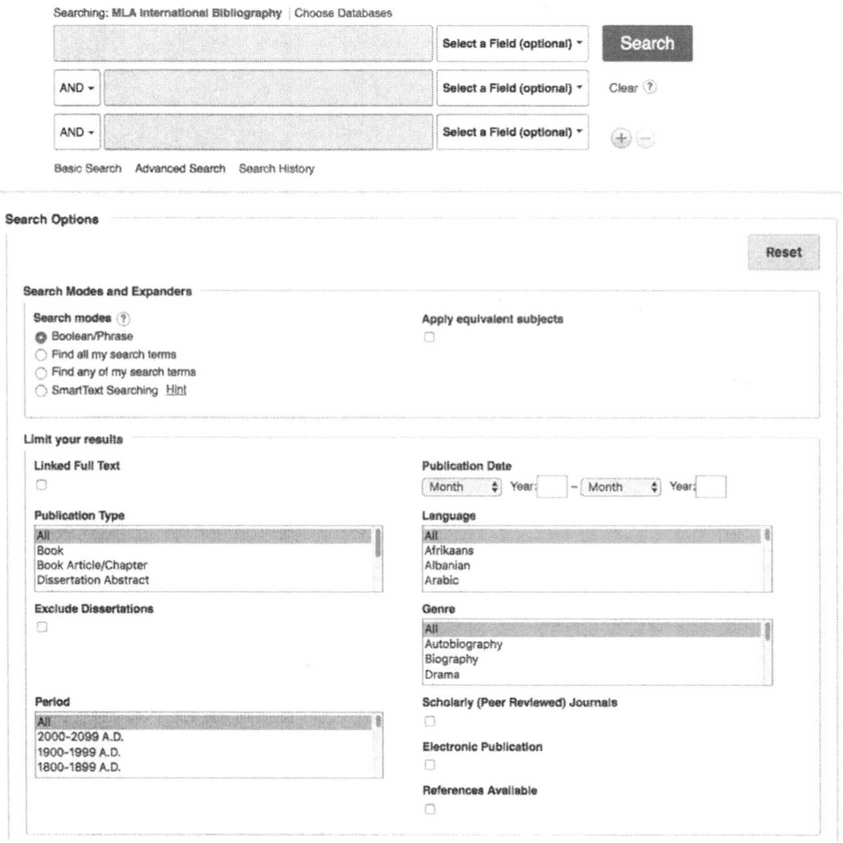

Fig. 19. Limiting your search

Fig. 20. Limiting your search to one journal

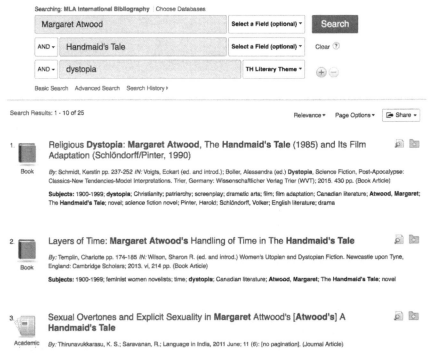

Fig. 21. Results for *Handmaid's Tale* AND *dystopia*

The Handmaid's Tale, you will retrieve records that contain the term in the title of the article or the title of the publication. If instead you use the drop-down menu to search for *dystopia* with the limiting field "Literary Theme," you will retrieve just those articles in which the author discusses dystopia in Atwood's work (fig. 21). One caveat to searching by fields like "Literary Theme" or "Scholarly Theory" is that you risk limiting your results too much. If you find that your search yields too little information, try doing a keyword search instead using alternate forms—that is, similar terms—and an OR to connect them: *dystopia* OR *dystopias* OR *dystopian* OR *dystopianism*. If that strategy doesn't work, check with your librarian for advice on other options.

Interdisciplinary Databases

EBSCO's *Academic Search* is a database that covers all subjects, not just literature or language studies. It also includes a variety of resources, such as newspapers, popular magazines, and **trade publications**, along with scholarly literature. The advantage of *Academic Search* is that it gives you access to information of immediate relevance or popular interest (a current film review in *Variety Magazine*, an article in the *New York Times* on a recent event) and scholarly articles on subjects outside literary criticism. If you want to identify articles on women's rights or gender inequality in the United States to supplement your thesis on *The Handmaid's Tale*, *Academic Search* is an excellent place to start.

The easiest way to begin is by doing a keyword search. The database will take these core terms that represent your topic and match them with the content in its universe. *Women's rights* produces over 15,000 results—far too many! In the results, you will see that the terms you entered are in bold font. Some are together (*women's rights*), but some are not, because a keyword search matches the terms you enter regardless of where they appear in the record. If you place quotation marks around the terms ("*women's rights*"), you will get 14,000 results, fewer but not much of an improvement.

You can limit your search to scholarly articles or to the most recent publications (fig. 22). Or you can add keywords. Adding "*United States*" in the second search box will limit the results to those items that have the phrase "United States" somewhere in the record. You have used the Boolean operator AND to narrow your results (fig. 23). Adding another term, *reproduction*, will narrow them further.

Including singular and plural spellings, synonyms, and variations of a word will help. For instance, you could use the phrase "*reproductive rights*" in addition to *reproduction*. The term *abortion* might be too specific or out of the scope of your thesis. Play around with your keyword searches in this way to get a sense of what will give you the best results. Using the Boolean operator OR to look for multiple terms at one time— *reproductive rights* OR *reproduction*—doubles the number of items retrieved (fig. 24). Truncation is another strategy. Use an asterisk to cover all variant possibilities in one search: *reproducti** will match on the words *reproduction, reproductive,* and *reproductive rights* all at one time (fig. 25).

Suppose that in your results list you have an article about migrant women in northwestern Mexico even though your search terms included the phrase "*United States*" and the phrase is absent in the subject terms

Fig. 22. Limiting your search to the most recent publications

at the bottom of the record. That means your keyword search matched the terms somewhere else in the record. There is a simple way to fix this problem of false hits: use the drop-down arrow to the right of the box with "*United States*" and move it from "Select a Field (Optional)" to "SU Subject Terms." Now when you search, "*United States*" must match as a subject heading, and there will be no article on any place other than the United States (fig. 26). If your library does not subscribe to EBSCO's *Academic Search* products, similar databases may be available to you, such as Gale's *Expanded Academic Index ASAP* and ProQuest's *Research Library*.

Depending on your library's subscription model, *JSTOR* and *Project MUSE* contain full-text articles from both scholarly journals and books. These tools contain peer-reviewed sources in all subject areas, so they are an excellent place to search for information on interdisciplinary

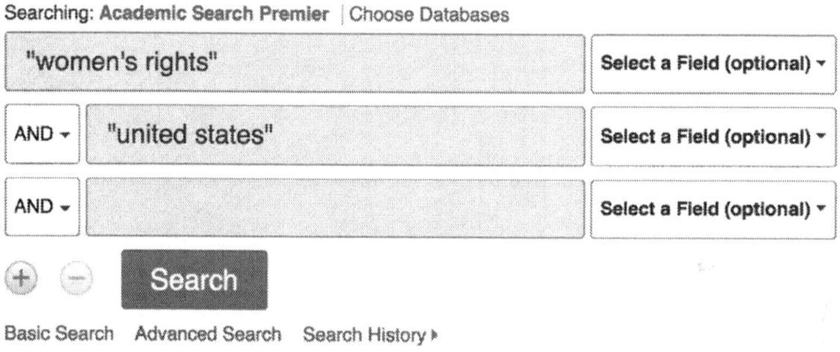

Fig. 23. Using AND to limit your search

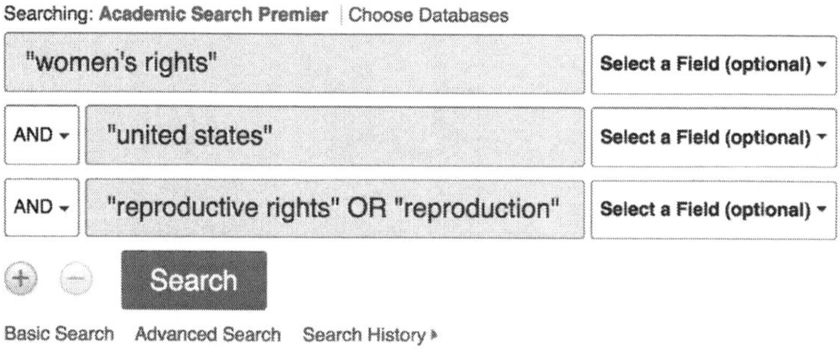

Fig. 24. Adding a field to limit your search further

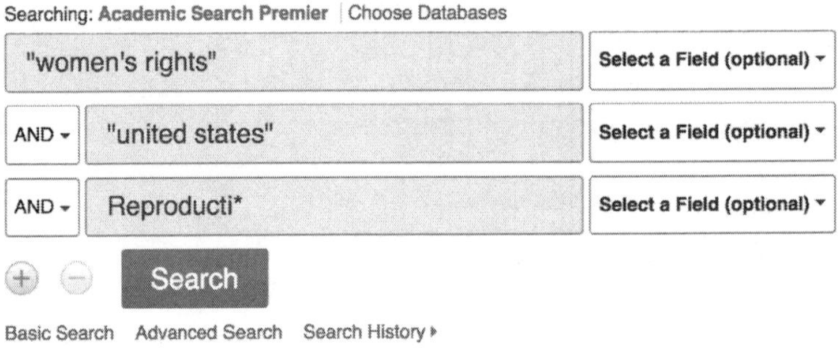

Searching: **Academic Search Premier** | Choose Databases

"women's rights"		Select a Field (optional) ▾
AND ▾	"united states"	Select a Field (optional) ▾
AND ▾	Reproducti*	Select a Field (optional) ▾

⊕ ⊖ **Search**

Basic Search   Advanced Search   Search History ▸

Fig. 25. Using truncation

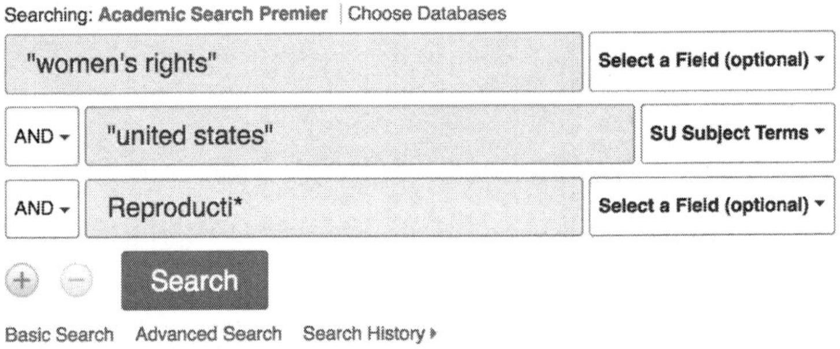

Searching: **Academic Search Premier** | Choose Databases

"women's rights"		Select a Field (optional) ▾
AND ▾	"united states"	SU Subject Terms ▾
AND ▾	Reproducti*	Select a Field (optional) ▾

⊕ ⊖ **Search**

Basic Search   Advanced Search   Search History ▸

Fig. 26. Using "SU Subject Terms"

topics. The most recent (published in the last two to five years) articles will not be available in *JSTOR*, because its primary purpose is to serve as an archive. For instance, the journal *Comparative Literature* is available from volume 1 (1949) through volume 63 (2011). In *Project MUSE*, a full-text resource of scholarly journals in the humanities and social sciences, book collections were added in 2012, so you can search both content from peer-reviewed journals and academic book publishers at the same time. Current issues of journals are available, but often the older issues are not. For instance, the journal *Comparative Literature Studies* is available only from volume 36 (1999) to the present. *JSTOR* and *Project MUSE* tend to be offered in larger research libraries, so check with your library to see if you have access to them.

4

Searching
the Internet

Today many people think that doing research means searching the Internet. Search engines, such as *Google*, *Bing*, and *Yahoo!*, are familiar to most people with access to the Internet. These tools have continually improved and are now easy to use, intuitive, and capable of presenting you with a very large set of results for almost any kind of search. Using the Internet for academic research, however, can be more complicated than it might initially seem.

As locating information has become easier, evaluating information has become more difficult. Remember that in academic research it is important not only to use information sources that are credible and trustworthy but also, most of the time, to use a specific type of source: scholarly and peer-reviewed. An enormous number of search results—often millions or tens of millions—can be overwhelming, a little like trying to drink through a fire hose. And most of what is contained in those millions of Web sites is either not relevant, not credible, or not scholarly, so using only the Internet will not give you a good idea of the sources that are available and appropriate to your topic. Another problem is that the filtering and sorting processes inevitably at play when you search the Internet are largely invisible and beyond your control. The **search algorithms** used by search engines like *Google* take into account factors such as your location, your preferences, your other activity on the Internet, and the overall popularity of Web sites, which can be influenced in various ways. These algorithms often exhibit bias based on factors such as gender, race, and ethnicity (Noble).

As discussed in chapters 2 and 3, there are library tools and databases available to you as an undergraduate student that are more precise and effective than Internet search engines when it comes to finding the scholarly, peer-reviewed sources you are generally expected to use in a college paper assignment; that give you more control over your search; and that offer content that is not available for free on the Internet. This does not mean, however, that information found on the Internet is inherently bad or unreliable or that you should never use a Web site as a source for your academic assignment. Whether or not it is appropriate for you to use nonscholarly content found on the Internet depends on the assignment and its requirements. If it is appropriate, you must still make sure to evaluate critically any information you find before using it. In this chapter, we discuss tools, strategies, and tips for making Internet research more precise and efficient and how to evaluate information no matter where it comes from.

Finding Scholarship on the Internet

The authors of this book do not intend to endorse one search engine over another, but the fact of the matter is that *Google Scholar* is the only search engine that has a robust interface for searching for scholarly articles. To search in *Google Scholar*, enter your keywords into the search field as you would for any Internet search. Since you are searching scholarly material, however, keep in mind the methods and strategies for keyword searching discussed in chapters 1 and 2. For example, use keywords that scholars are likely to use when discussing your topic. Use quotation marks and asterisks and connect your keywords with Boolean operators, and there will be less irrelevant content for you to wade through. Suppose you're doing research for an assignment on Charlotte Perkins Gilman's story "The Yellow Wallpaper" and your topic is about the symbolism in it. If you search for *the yellow wallpaper symbolism* in *Google Scholar*, you'll receive over nine thousand results; if you search for *"the yellow wallpaper"* AND *symbolism*, you'll receive about 2,600, still a large set but more relevant to your topic because you've ensured they all include *"the yellow wallpaper"* as a phrase.

The results screen in *Google Scholar* looks slightly different from that for a standard *Google* search. Your results will still be in the middle of the page with those identifiable blue links and short descriptions underneath, but you will be given additional information. Notice the text in green directly underneath the link to the article: as in a library database, it includes the author's name, the name of the journal that published the article, the year it was published, and sometimes the name of the database where it can be found. Sometimes you can click to a PDF document of the article, though it is often stripped of identifying information. With the information about author and publication provided in the search results, you can verify the credentials of the article, review the journal to make sure that it is peer-reviewed and deals with the field you are researching, and create the citation for your works-cited list. Underneath the short blurb about the article, there is a row of links to other useful tools (fig. 27).

When you have your first set of results, *Google Scholar* presents you with options to narrow your results further. These limiters are on the left-hand side of the page. You can choose the type of document (under "Articles" or "Case Law") and the time range of publication. You can sort

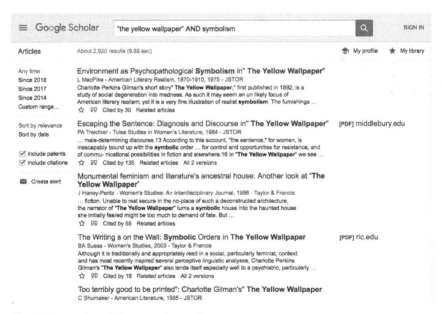

Fig. 27. *Google Scholar* search results

your results by date or by relevance. There are not as many options in *Google Scholar* as are available to you in a library database, but with those that are available you can limit or expand your results in the same way you would in a library database, as discussed in chapters 2 and 3.

When you use *Google Scholar*, there will sometimes be sources among your results that may not fulfill the requirements of your research assignment—for example, book reviews and dissertations. A quick way to find out whether what you are looking at is an academic article is to look for the name of the journal. If you are not familiar with the scholarly journals in the field, you can learn about the journal from a quick Internet search or in your library database. Book reviews are tricky because they are often published in peer-reviewed journals, typically at the end of an issue after all the articles. Because of where they are published, *Google Scholar*—and many library databases as well—sometimes mistakenly includes them as peer-reviewed, scholarly articles. Look for the word "review" somewhere in the search result, header, title, or first paragraph of the document. Look also at the length: a book review is usually much shorter than a scholarly article. If still in doubt, read the first few paragraphs. If it seems like a summary of a book or sounds like someone giving an opinion on a book instead of analyzing or interpreting it critically, then it is probably a book review. A book review has its uses in academic research, especially if it is contemporary to the author, as discussed in chapter 5, but it is not the same thing as a scholarly, peer-reviewed journal article.

A **dissertation** is a long paper written to meet a requirement of a doctoral program, which means that the author is a student—an advanced student, admittedly, but still a student. Although dissertations are reviewed by a committee of professors, they are not published unless they are reworked and explicitly submitted for publication after the student receives a PhD. Dissertations look and sound scholarly, but many professors will not accept them for research assignments that require peer-reviewed sources.

How will you know if you have come across a dissertation in your *Google Scholar* search? Look for the publisher. If it is a dissertation, the publisher will probably be the university that the student was attending. When in doubt, do some research into the publisher and look for a mission or scope note, often found on an "About" page. Even if you cannot use dissertations as cited sources in your research paper, they can still be useful to you in your research. Since they are written by students studying to become academic scholars, they have extensive bibliographies and often literature reviews, which summarize all the scholarship on the topic that had been published up to that point. These two elements of a dissertation can point you in the direction of peer-reviewed books and articles that will fit your professor's requirements.

Two useful tools that *Google Scholar* has that many library databases do not are the "Cited by" and "Related Articles" options. Links for these are below the blurb for the article on the results screen (fig. 27). You can click on "Cited by" to find other articles that are related to your topic, just as an article's works-cited list can point you to other books and articles relevant to your research—this method of research is called **citation chaining**. The "Cited by" option lists articles that have cited the article at hand, which means that they were published after the article was published. Used together, the works-cited section of your article and the "Cited by" list should give you a good sense of the scholarly literature on the topic your article discusses—both before and since its publication. Note that a list of relevant articles created by a researcher (i.e., the works-cited list) will be of greater value to you than that produced by an algorithm, on the principle that a human being can make more nuanced connections between topics than a computer can.

Accessing Scholarship Online

You may find the Internet in general and *Google Scholar* in particular to be more familiar and convenient to use than your library's databases, but be aware that scholarly materials are not, for the most part, available for free online to anyone who wants to read them. College and university libraries pay for scholarly books—both those in print and electronic—and pay subscription fees to scholarly journals and database vendors in order to be able to make scholarly literature available to students. You have already paid for access to this literature, because part of the library's budget comes from your tuition dollars.

The Internet, on the other hand, does not know that you are an enrolled student, so often you will be taken to a page that asks you to pay for access to an article. Or, if you are interested in a book, you will be able to view only a snippet of it and be directed to a site where you can buy it. The fee to access an article can be anywhere from twenty-five to ninety dollars, and scholarly books sometimes cost more. But you should not have to pay for any of these materials: let your library obtain for you any book or article you find on *Google Scholar* or the open Internet.

Thankfully, *Google Scholar* does provide a way to link articles found through its search directly to your campus library's holdings. This linking may happen automatically on campus computers, depending on your college or university, but you may have to enable it. Go into *Google Scholar*'s settings and look for "Library Links." If you need help connecting *Google Scholar* to your college or university library or if you need an article you find on *Google Scholar* that your library does not have access to, ask a librarian for help. To access a scholarly book that you find in *Google Scholar* or from a general Internet search, do a search for it in your library's discovery system (see chapter 2).

There is an exception to this discussion of online access to scholarly materials: **open access**. As the term suggests, such scholarship is available online for free, immediately, and for use by anyone (see SPARC at sparcopen.org/open-access). In your Internet search you may come across open-access books or articles of scholarly literary criticism. These materials are peer-reviewed, just like their counterparts published by traditional journals or book presses, but it can be difficult to tell the difference between them and other Internet sources. Look for the phrase "open access" on the site and look for the universal symbol for open access, the open lock (fig. 28). Look for an "About" page for information

Fig. 28. "Open Access" symbol

about the mission of the publisher, the scope of what it publishes, and whether or not the material it publishes is peer-reviewed. If you are not sure whether or not material is open-access scholarship, ask a librarian.

Searching Smarter: Search Engine Advanced Tools

If your research assignment allows you to make use of sources outside the scholarly literature, you will likely want to search the Internet. We are confident we do not need to instruct you on how to do a basic search, but you may not know that most search engines have an advanced search interface or set of tools that function very much like the tools in a library database. Access to them depends on which search engine you use. They are sometimes hard to find, because links to them have been moved around and downgraded fairly frequently by search engines in recent years (Notess 43, 45).

Google and *Yahoo!* both have forms for advanced searching that lay out all the options available in one place, and a quick search on the main search engine page for "Google advanced search" or "Yahoo advanced search" will result in links to these pages.[1] The forms allow you to use Boolean operators to expand or limit your results. You can use them to search for exact phrases, number ranges, languages, regions or countries of the world, the last time the site was updated, the domain of the site (.com, .org, .edu, .gov), and more. Most of the advanced search options offered on the *Google* and *Yahoo!* forms can also be used in the basic search boxes for these search engines, as well as with other search engines like *Bing* and *DuckDuckGo*, by entering the necessary symbols or characters along with your keywords. The symbols and characters needed for each advanced operation are specified either on the advanced search forms themselves (for *Google* and *Yahoo!*) or on Web pages dedicated to listing all these symbols and characters (for *Bing* and *DuckDuckGo*).[2] The symbols and characters range from the simple to the complex. For instance, a simple search might make use of quotation marks around a phrase (e.g., *"The Yellow Wallpaper"*). A complex search might make use of a series of parentheses and Boolean operators—for example, (*"The Yellow Wallpaper"* OR *"Charlotte Perkins Gilman"*) AND (*feminism* OR *women*).[3]

You will see the biggest difference in your results between an advanced search and a basic search when you are researching a topic that is controversial or commonly discussed in popular culture. For example, entering *Mark Twain censorship* in the basic *Google* search box will result in a first page of results made up mainly of quotation Web sites, pop culture Web sites, and opinion pieces from various media outlets—and most will date back to 2011 (fig. 29). They will probably not be acceptable for an academic research paper. Using the *Google* Advanced Search Form to make some changes to your search yields a more promising set of results. You can use it to specify that you want recent information (e.g., from the past year) and information only from educational Web

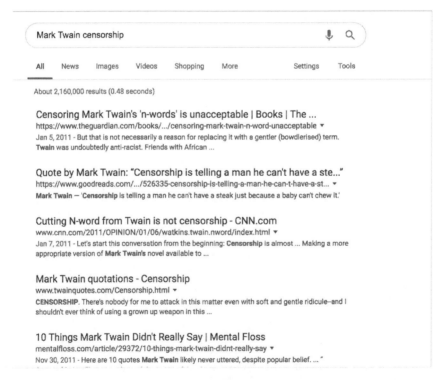

Fig. 29. Internet search results for *Mark Twain censorship*

sites (i.e., with .edu domains). Using these options will not ensure that the results are what you are looking for or that they are acceptable to your professor, but you will have more control over your search and be less at the mercy of the search engine's algorithm. The result of these two changes on our search for *Mark Twain censorship* is a completely different set of results on the first page (fig. 30).

Evaluating Internet Sources

It is important for you to know how to control and change your Internet search results because not all Web pages are suitable for academic work. Suitability is something you can intuit: looking at a page, you get a gut

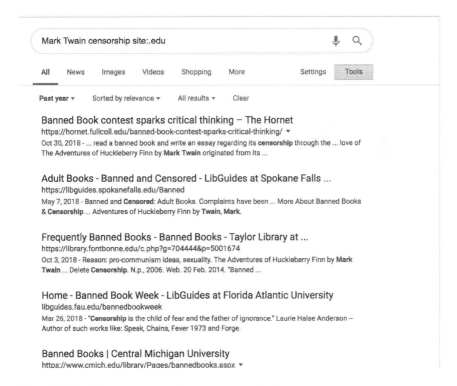

Fig. 30. Limiting your search to recent .edu sites

feeling about whether or not your professor will want you to use it as a source for your research assignment. But how can you be sure? What criteria cause this gut reaction? Examining that gut response can make you aware of the criteria, and then you can consciously and consistently apply them to any Web page.

There are many different models and checklists out there to help you evaluate a Web site. They all have their merits, but sometimes running through a checklist can turn off your critical thinking skills. You need those skills, because in today's information landscape there are no easy answers. You must stay alert and engaged with the information you are consuming, whether it is a *Facebook* post from your uncle or an academic article written by an expert. Therefore, instead of giving you a checklist to run through, we would rather that you ask yourself questions. They might be:

What Is This?

Take a moment, before you dive in, to figure out exactly what it is you are looking at. It is online, yes, but so is almost everything these days. Take in the whole page, the URL, the logos, and the images. Skim the text. Is this a news Web site? a blog? a PDF file? Where did it come from, and where is it hosted? Is it paid for by a company, an association, or advertisers? The Web site of a college or university? The Web site of a publisher or vendor? Is it located in a database of some sort?

If it is a news Web site, you will want to know who wrote the article, where the writer got the information, and what experience or credentials give the writer expertise on the topic. Does the article employ standards of journalistic objectivity, or is the writer giving an opinion (known as an op-ed)? It is not that one of these is good and one is bad, but knowing which it is should inform your decision about if and how to use the information it presents. If it is a scholarly article in a database, you will want to see whether or not the journal is peer-reviewed and in your field, and you may want to learn more about the scholar and the scholar's credentials. If it is a PDF, you will want to figure out where it came from—from a scholarly journal, or is it perhaps a term paper that another undergraduate scanned and put online?

What Is My Initial Response to This Web Site?

After using the Internet for many years, you have developed a sense of which Web sites are trustworthy and which are not. Go with that gut reaction—it is probably leading you in the right direction. But take the time to examine your reaction and put it into words. **Confirmation bias** is a normal response: you tend to believe something that confirms what you already think to be true or supports an opinion you already hold, and you tend not to accept information that goes against what you already believe. But when you do research, the whole point is to learn new things! So take a step back and ask yourself why your initial reaction was either positive or negative.

Does your gut tell you that this site will be a good source for your research? Why or why not? Do the ads on the site make you skeptical? What about them gives you that impression? Does the fact that the URL ends with a .gov or .org make you confident? On today's Internet, there are many different domains, and most of them (including .org and .edu) are available to anybody or any organization, so you need to dig deeper. Does the tone of the writing suggest that the writer is expressing an opinion? What is that opinion based on, evidence and research or other people's opinions? Questions like these should lead to other questions, and you continue to move along.

Who Is Responsible for This Web Site?

There should be an author credited on the Web page you are considering. If so, who is it? What are the person's credentials? What experiences or training or education makes the person an expert or **authority** on the subject? If an opinion is given, what reason do you have to trust it? Take a look at the evidence cited and links included—does it all seem solid? If the author is telling you about research that someone else has done, how can you check that research? Are there references you can use, links that take you to the source of the information? Use such links to verify claims as you would use references in an article.

Besides the author, who bears responsibility for the content? Who published the article? Is it a news outlet? a nonprofit organization? a business or company? an academic journal? What credentials does the publisher have? If the publisher is an organization, can you look up some of the people in the organization? Often information about them can be found on an "About" or "Mission" page. You can also search the Internet for the people involved in the site. What else have they published? What is their reputation? What other sites or outlets do they write for?

When Was This Web Site Written or Published?

Does the Web site have a date on it? If the article or page you are considering does not have one, try looking for the date when the page or site was last revised—that might give you an idea of how old the article or page is. Given the time it was written, is the article still relevant today? If you cannot find a date for a Web site or Web page, is there a way to tell, without the date, that the information on it is still relevant?

The answer to these questions will depend on your topic and the field you are researching. Research and information in literature do not become obsolete as quickly as they do in other disciplines—*Moby-Dick* is still *Moby-Dick* whether someone wrote about it this year or fifty years ago. It is usually acceptable therefore to use literary essays written many years ago. But the acceptability can vary by topic.

Keep asking questions until you feel confident that your evaluation process has led you to a decision about whether or not to use the source for your assignment. The point at which this happens will be different for different people and for different sources.

Evaluating Library Sources

Perhaps the complexities of searching for academically appropriate content on the Internet have made you decide to use your library's databases instead. Searching in these databases means that you can definitely rely on the sources you find. . . right? Not necessarily! The need for you to evaluate sources does not disappear because you are using library databases and scholarly books and articles instead of Web pages. You should make sure that every source of information you use, no matter what it is or where it comes from, is both trustworthy and a good fit for your current context—keeping in mind that no source is the right choice in every circumstance. Many library databases these days include records for all types of information—things you will also find on the open Internet, such as magazines, newspapers, and *Wikipedia* articles—and some will not be acceptable to your professor. Scholarly articles and books also need scrutiny. Articles are retracted regularly for mistakes or outright fraud, though this retraction is more common in the sciences than in the humanities and other disciplines (Fox 69).

All information sources, including scholarly sources, are written by human beings, and human beings, even those with PhDs and impressive credentials, are fallible. Their work may go through highly rigorous peer review, but not all research has equal merit. Therefore you should always evaluate. Is a source trustworthy? Is a piece of information credible? Is the author of a work an authority? Is the work relevant to your topic? Is it good for your purpose or only adequate? Though it may be tempting to settle for the first source you find that has information on your topic, your research papers will always be better if you apply a critical eye to your options and choose the source (be that an article, book, or Web page) that is the best fit for your argument or interpretation.

Notes

1. As of the writing of this volume, the URL for *Google*'s Advanced Search Form is www.google.com/advanced_search and the URL for *Yahoo!*'s Advanced Search Form is www.yahoo.com/r/so.

2. As of the writing of this volume, a list of search refinements for *Google* can be found at support.google.com/websearch/answer/2466433. The Advanced Operator Reference page for *Bing* is located at msdn.microsoft.com/en-us/library/ff795620.aspx. The Search Syntax page for *DuckDuckGo* is located at duck.co/help/results/syntax.

3. The AND in this example search is unnecessary in *Google*, because that search engine assumes that a space between words that are not enclosed in quotations marks means "and." In other search engines, you will need the AND. In any case, including it will help you keep track of your more complicated searches.

Works Cited

Fox, Mary Frank. "Fraud, Ethics, and the Disciplinary Contexts of Science and Scholarship." *The American Sociologist*, vol. 21, no. 1, 1990, pp. 67–71.

Noble, Safiya Umoja. "Google Search: Hyper-visibility as a Means of Rendering Black Women and Girls Invisible." *InVisible Culture*, 29 Oct. 2013, ivc.lib.rochester.edu/google-search-hyper-visibility-as-a-means-of-rendering-black-women-and-girls-invisible/.

Notess, Greg R. "Advanced Search in Retreat." *Information Today*, www.infotoday.com/online/mar12/On-the-Net-Advanced-Search-in-Retreat.shtml.

5

Finding Reviews

In your research you will sometimes need to use a book review. As discussed in chapter 4, book reviews are not peer-reviewed sources, but they can still be useful for certain types of assignments. For instance, your instructor may have asked you to investigate how a nineteenth-century novel was received when it was first published. Or you may be writing a paper about a film or play that was released recently and want to see critics' responses to it.

Most reviews, written shortly after a work is published or performed, pass judgment on its worthiness. They typically appear in popular magazines, book trade publications, and newspapers. Reviews of academic books, written by scholars in peer-reviewed journals, take longer to appear, often a year or more after the book is published. Reviews of creative works in scholarly journals usually have a more critical focus than their counterparts in popular magazines and newspapers, but they are rarely, if ever, subject to the peer-review process. Because academic book reviews published in scholarly journals typically contain both a summary and a critical evaluation of the content, they can help place the work in a larger context. For secondary sources, a good academic reviewer will demonstrate where a book stands in the scholarly literature and what contribution, if any, it makes to the field.

Criticism, on the other hand, is usually written a significant amount of time after a book is published. Critical articles about a literary work typically focus on a theme or technique used by the author. Scholars often compare two or more authors or works to evaluate, analyze, or interpret. Book-length works may go beyond the examination of one literary work and consider an author's writings as a whole. Scholars often use a literary theory—psychoanalytic criticism or reader-response criticism, for example—to examine a work. For more information about the various schools of criticism, see the Purdue OWL (Online Writing Lab) Web site or the *Johns Hopkins Guide to Literary Theory and Criticism*. More information about these resources is available in the appendix.

EBSCO's *Academic Search*, discussed in chapter 3, is an excellent resource for finding book reviews, from the 1980s on, published in popular magazines, trade publications, and scholarly journals. Let's say that you are interested in researching a new novel by the author Zadie Smith. You have searched the *MLA International Bibliography* and can find no criticism of her *Swing Time* (2016). A quick keyword search in *Academic Search* for "*Swing Time*" limited to document type "Book Review" turns up fifty-nine records (figs. 31 and 32). Most of the results are reviews from trade

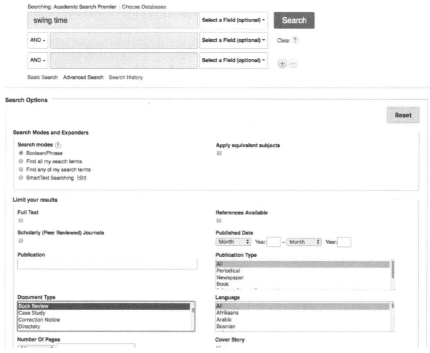

Fig. 31. Searching for book reviews of *Swing Time*

publications and popular magazines like *The New York Times Book Review*, the *London Review of Books, Publisher's Weekly, Harper's Magazine*, and the *New Yorker*. But there is a review from a scholarly journal, the *Virginia Quarterly Review*. If your research assignment requires the use of theater or film reviews, you will find those also in *Academic Search*. Select the appropriate document type option on the main search screen ("Film Review" or "Entertainment Review") and search for the title in order to locate reviews of your film or play. If your library does not have access to *Academic Search,* a few other options that work equally well are Gale's *Expanded Academic Index ASAP* and ProQuest's *Research Library*. Your library may have a subscription to a database that focuses on reviews, like *Book Review Index Plus*.

Sometimes the only option for finding a review is a newspaper. Newspapers, unlike magazines, are published daily. If your instructor accepts the use of newspapers in your research project, a good database

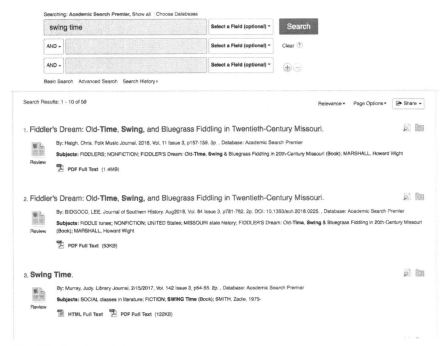

Fig. 32. Results of the search

is *Nexis Uni*. Formerly known as *LexisNexis Academic Complete, Nexis Uni* is a full-text database of over 15,000 news, business, and legal sources. The newspapers are published throughout the world but are mostly in English. Other newspaper databases that may be available at your library are ProQuest's *Newsstream* and *Access World News* from Readex.

Sometimes you may be faced with the challenge of finding a contemporary review of an older work, like Charlotte Brontë's *Jane Eyre* or Mark Twain's *Adventures of Huckleberry Finn—contemporary* here meaning written soon after the novel's publication. Such a search can be difficult to do, as the databases we have discussed cover resources only back to the early 1980s. You will need different databases for reviews written before the late twentieth century. For *Jane Eyre*, you would need a review from 1847. An excellent resource for locating magazine articles and book re-

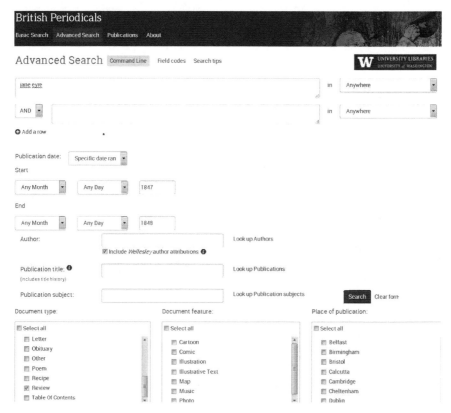

Fig. 33. Limiting your search for *Jane Eyre* by date range

views from nineteenth-century England is ProQuest's *British Periodicals*, which provides full-text access to over five hundred British periodicals published from the seventeenth century to the early twenty-first. The advanced search screen allows you to search for items on "*Jane Eyre*" and limit your results in a variety of ways. For instance, you could search for "*Jane Eyre*" in the date range "1847 to 1848" and for the document type "Review" (fig. 33). This search brings up twenty results, all with full text available with one click (fig. 34).

If you are looking for early reviews of an American literary work, ProQuest has a United States counterpart to *British Periodicals* called *American Periodicals Series Online*. It contains digitized images of American magazines and journals published from the colonial days to the beginning of the twentieth century. Two other databases that are useful for finding older reviews are *Humanities and Social Sciences Index Retrospective* (1907–84) and the *Reader's Guide Retrospective* (1890–1982).

There are also offline options for finding older reviews of a literary work. The *Combined Retrospective Index to Book Reviews in Humanities Journals,* a multivolume print index to book reviews published during the years 1802–1974, is one of the best resources available. Search

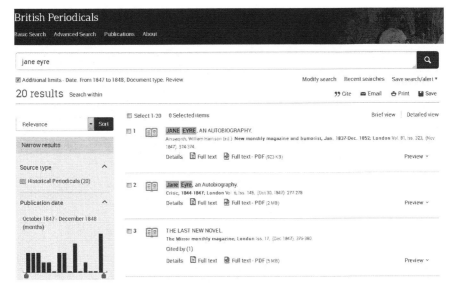

Fig. 34. Results of the search

your library's discovery system or catalog to see where this resource is located, then go to the shelf and find the alphabetically arranged volume that covers your author and look under the entry (by the author's last name). The volume contains a list of reviews that were published for all the author's works, arranged by title. Your library's catalog will tell you whether or not your library has access to the magazine or journal in which the review was published.

One final strategy for locating reviews of an older work is to consult a bibliography on the author. Most book-length bibliographies include book reviews on an author's works. A quick way to discover if a bibliography is available is to search your library's catalog or the *MLA International Bibliography*. A search for *Charlotte Brontë* AND *bibliography* in

---

Jane Eyre — Nineteenth-Century Reviews
Listed in Chronological Order

A49   Anon. A review of *Jane Eyre. Spectator,* Nov. 6, 1847, pp. 1074-1075.

        A hostile review, of which Charlotte Brontë says to her editor (see A48): "The critique . . . gives that view of the book which will naturally be taken by a certain class of mind."

A50   Anon. A review of *Jane Eyre. Economist,* 5 (Nov. 27, 1847), 1376.

        Praises the beginning of the novel, not the romance between Jane and Mr. Rochester.

A51   Anon. "The Literary Examiner." A review of *Jane Eyre. Examiner,* Nov. 27, 1847, pp. 756-757.

        Jane Eyre is deemed to be a "very clever book," one of "decided power." The style is judged to be "resolute, straight-forward, and to the purpose," though here and there "rude and uncultivated." On the whole, a very favorable review.

A52   Anon. "New Books." A review of *Jane Eyre. Douglas Jerrold's Shilling Magazine,* 6 (Nov. 1847), 473-474.

        A favorable review comments on the author's artistic sensitivity.

A53   [Lewes, George Henry]. "Recent Novels: French and English." A review of *Jane Eyre. Fraser's Magazine,* 36 (Dec. 1847), 690-694.

        This influential literary gentleman finds "deep, significant reality" as "the great characteristic of the book." He suggests that

10

Fig. 35. Chronological list of reviews of *Jane Eyre*

your library discovery system or catalog, for example, will likely yield a book by Anne Passel called *Charlotte and Emily Brontë: An Annotated Bibliography*. If you look at the table of contents for this bibliography, you will see that the author divides the sections into primary and secondary materials. Among the secondary materials are book reviews. Pages 10 through 16 list reviews of *Jane Eyre* from 1847 to 1885 (fig. 35). Check your local library catalog to see which review sources are available in the collection.

6

Using Contextual Primary Sources

Research assignments in English and American literature classes often require that you find secondary resources to support an argument or thesis. We discussed in earlier chapters how to find literary criticism published in journals and books, and how to find reviews for creative works written too recently to have scholarly criticism published about them or written so long ago that specialized tools are needed to see how a contemporary audience received them. These are all examples of secondary sources. Secondary sources analyze and make claims or arguments about a primary source. In literary studies, they are typically about a particular novel, poem, or other creative work. They provide context for and a critical analysis of the work, as seen through the eyes of the scholar writing the journal article, book chapter, or dissertation. Instructors will sometimes ask that you also incorporate primary sources to support your arguments. What is a primary source, and why is it important for understanding a literary work? How do you discover and locate primary sources in the library? How can you tell if what you're looking at is a primary source? Finally, how do you use a primary source to support your thesis? All these questions will be addressed in this chapter.

What Is a Primary Source?

Simply put, primary sources are the artifacts that secondary sources analyze. In literature they fall into two categories: the creative work itself, both in published and manuscript form; materials that were written or published during the author's lifetime, such as diaries, letters to friends or publishers, or an autobiography, or not written by the author but available while the author was alive and writing. Examples of these types of artifacts are newspaper and magazine articles, photographs, sound recordings, and videos. Primary sources can help you understand the context of a literary work, because they create a picture of what was going on during the author's time. People are influenced by what happens in their life, whether the influence is personal or affects the larger community around them. As a student of literature, you should be aware of an author's environment to understand the themes or issues reflected in the author's works. Being able to discover and incorporate primary sources will add another dimension to your analysis of a literary work or theme.

Discovering a primary source can be difficult, depending on the author, historical event, or time period you are researching. One question to consider before you begin your research is, What resources were available at the time in question? For instance, if you're researching Shakespeare, were newspapers published and readily accessible to people then? Did Shakespeare write personal diaries or letters? If so, you can imagine that these resources are extremely rare today and tightly controlled by a few special libraries, given their age and Shakespeare's importance. In the past, literary scholars had to travel to a select number of libraries in England or the United States in order to view and utilize resources like these for their work. With the rise of the Internet, however, libraries and commercial publishers began digitizing collections that were once restricted to only a few people. Because digitization is expensive, many primary source collections are provided only through commercial publishers at a cost to libraries. For those interested in an author like Shakespeare, a good example is ProQuest's *Early English Books Online* (*EEBO*). *EEBO* contains digital facsimile page images of virtually every work printed in England, Ireland, Scotland, and Wales from 1473 to 1700. You can view the pages of six different editions of *Hamlet* printed from 1603 to 1637. Many libraries are also digitizing collections with the goal of making them freely available on the Web. The British Library is one, and it has many amazing collections to explore, such as *Shakespeare in Quarto*, a digitized collection of 107 copies of the twenty-one plays by Shakespeare printed before 1642. The images in this resource are in many cases better than those available in *EEBO*.

Periodicals as Primary Sources

A resource like *EEBO* is great for seeing rare first editions of books published during the early phase of printing in England. But what if you are interested in seeing articles published in periodicals in the nineteenth century? Traditionally, there have been two major methods to achieve this goal: use an index to periodical literature that covers the decade or century you're researching; use the bibliography of a secondary resource on your topic to see what primary sources are being cited. These methods are still valid today. But depending on the date range you are researching, options for using an index may be limited. There are a handful of tools available for magazine content from the nineteenth century, including *Poole's Index to Periodical Literature* (1802–1907) and *The Wellesley Index to Victorian Periodicals* (1824–1900). These indexes only gather the basic information about articles published in a magazine (i.e., citations); they do not contain full-text images of the articles themselves. If you are using such a resource, you must perform a second step: searching your library's discovery system or catalog to see if the periodical you need is in its collection. Fortunately we now have an easier way to access full-text articles from historical and current newspapers and magazines: online archives of periodicals. *British Periodicals Online* contains five hundred titles published from the seventeenth to the early twenty-first century; *American Periodicals Online* contains over 1,500 titles published from the colonial period to the early twentieth century; *The London Times* contains periodicals from 1785 to 2009; and *The New York Times* contains them from 1851 to 2013. Because these are available only by subscription, check your library to see if you have access.

Using Primary Sources in Literary Research

Let's walk through a few examples of how to find primary sources by using Harriet Beecher Stowe's *Uncle Tom's Cabin*, regarded as one of the major forces behind the abolitionist movement in the United States during the nineteenth century. The novel's appraisal has been mixed in the twentieth and twenty-first centuries, but when it was published in 1852, it brought widespread attention to the horrible reality of slavery in the United States. It has been argued that the work contributed to the start of the Civil War in 1861. What if any effect did slavery have on Stowe personally? This is the type of question related to a literary work and author that can be answered using primary sources.

A little digging in *Oxford Reference Online* reveals that the Fugitive Slave Law was passed by the United States Congress on 18 September 1850, a couple of years before the publication of Stowe's novel. The law was enacted as part of the Compromise of 1850 between Southern slaveholder states and Northern free states and was a blow to abolitionists like Stowe. Searching *American Periodicals Online* for the phrase "*fugitive slave law*" and limiting the author field to "Stowe" brings up sixteen results (fig. 36). You can further limit your search to a year, such as 1850, but since there is only a small number of items that match, you can simply browse the existing set of sixteen. One article in particular stands out, Stowe's "The Freeman's Dream: A Parable," published in the *New York Evangelist* on 15 August 1850 (fig. 37). In this article Stowe admonishes the United States government for putting civil law above the laws of God. Quotes from it would be evidence for your research paper that

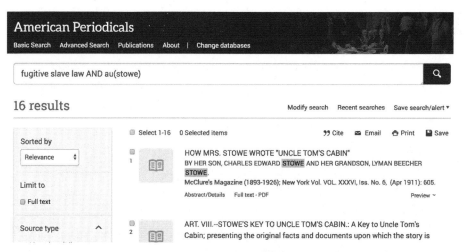

Fig. 36. Results for *fugitive slave law* AND *Stowe*

Stowe disagreed with the idea of compromising on slavery, evidence that you would not have had without the use of a primary source. Finally, keep in mind that a tried-and-true method for identifying primary sources on a topic is to make note of the sources scholars are quoting or incorporating in their work. Mining the bibliographies of books and articles (i.e., citation chaining) can be an excellent means of finding more information.

Finding Primary Sources through a Library Database or Catalog

In addition to using primary source documents available online, you can search your local library's discovery system or catalog. Begin by finding letters or diaries written by Stowe or those close to her. You do

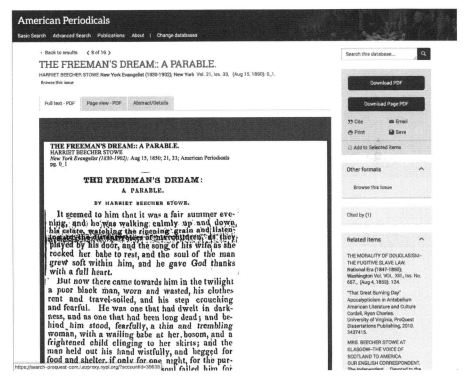

Fig. 37. One result is the text of Stowe's "The Freeman's Dream"

not need the actual handwritten letters; it is common to find personal correspondence collected and published in book form, usually after the author is deceased. A quick way to locate this information is to search your library catalog using the keywords *Harriet Beecher Stowe* AND *correspondence*. Such a search in a library discovery system or catalog finds the book: *Life and Letters of Harriet Beecher Stowe* (fig. 38). Other keywords you can use are *"personal narratives"* or *diaries*. Searching for *diaries* surfaces a book called *Harriet Beecher Stowe in Europe: The Journal of Charles Beecher*, which is a collection of correspondence and diaries compiled by Stowe's husband, Charles Edward Stowe (fig. 39). Typically, such collections of letters include an index. Use the index to find entries that mention or refer to the issue you are researching, in this case slavery. Another avenue to explore is locating documents on slavery that were written during Stowe's time. Using the keywords *slavery* AND *United States* AND *sources* to search the library database finds a book by Louis Filler called *Slavery in the United States of America*. This work includes the texts of key speeches and publications written by

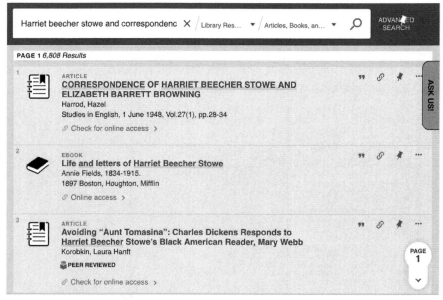

Fig. 38. Results for *Harriet Beecher Stowe* AND *correspondence*

important people at the time who were either opposed to or in favor of slavery.

Stowe was exposed to many of these materials, and they could have influenced her thinking and her choice of characters or themes in *Uncle Tom's Cabin*. Adding the keyword *sources* to your search will single out published collections of primary sources. Your library may or may not have the specific books described here, but the strategies you would use to find them are the same regardless of the library's collection. Also, remember that libraries share materials, so you should be able to request a book through interlibrary loan if your library does not own it.

Finding Primary Sources through the Internet

When searching for primary sources either in a library database or on the Internet, start by looking for specific people, places, or things associated with your topic. Using the phrase *"primary sources"* to search

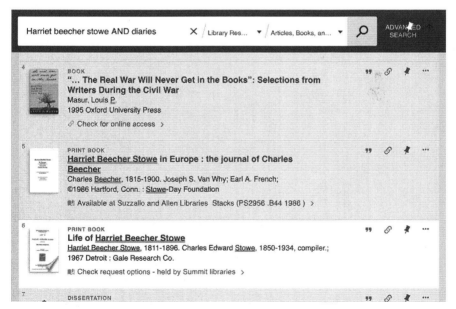

Fig. 39. Results for *Harriet Beecher Stowe* AND *diaries*

may not be a successful strategy. Using terms like *archive* or phrases like *"digital collection"* or *"digital library"* in addition to your author or topic may be more effective. Examine closely the host or sponsor of the sites you consider to make sure they are from trustworthy publishers or organizations. A good rule of thumb is to go with resources produced by major research institutions and libraries.

Good places to search for American historical documents are the *Digital Public Library of America* (dp.la/) and the *Library of Congress Digital Collections* (loc.gov/collections/). For primary documents on Stowe, a search in an Internet search engine like *Google* using the terms *Uncle Tom's Cabin digital collections* (AND is generally not needed when you use an Internet search engine) results in the site Uncle Tom's Cabin *and American Culture: A Multi-media Archive* (utc.iath.virginia.edu/). This archive, produced and maintained by the University of Virginia, is a portal to a variety of both primary and secondary documents on Stowe's novel and its portrayal of slavery in the United States. You can browse collections of reviews and responses to the novel from pro- and antislavery perspectives, as well as from a Christian perspective. Also available are contemporary reviews published in American periodicals; responses from the African American community, including those from key figures like Frederick Douglass; and proslavery responses from newspapers originating in Charleston, New Orleans, Richmond, and other United States cities.

If you are interested in looking more broadly at primary sources on the issue of slavery in the United States, there are many digitized archival collections available from libraries across the country. Searching *Google* with the terms *antislavery movement United States archive* yields *Antislavery Pamphlet Collection*, a resource at the University of Massachusetts Amherst Libraries (scua.library.umass.edu/umarmot/antislavery/). This site contains several hundred printed pamphlets and books pertaining to slavery and antislavery efforts in New England during the time period 1725–1911. Among the documents are speeches, sermons, and publications of organizations such as the American Anti-Slavery Society and the American Colonization Society.

Another way to understand the issue of slavery is to look at some of the primary documents from the slave trade. *American Slavery Documents* at Duke University Libraries (repository.duke.edu/dc/americanslavery docs) is an assortment of legal and personal documents designed to shed light on the everyday details of the lives and deaths of enslaved African Americans during the antebellum and early reconstruction periods. The types of materials included in the collection are bills of sale, emancipation notes, bonds, and auction notices.

Other sites that may be useful for researching *Uncle Tom's Cabin* or slavery in the United States are *Born in Slavery: Slave Narratives from the Federal Writers' Project, 1936 to 1938* (www.loc.gov/collections/slave-nar ratives-from-the-federal-writers-project-1936-to-1938/about-this-col lection/) and *The Abolition of the Slave Trade* (abolition.nypl.org/home/). *Born in Slavery* is a collection from the Library of Congress that contains more than 2,300 first-person accounts of slavery and five hundred black-and-white photographs of people who were formerly enslaved. *The Abolition of the Slave Trade* is a New York Public Library site offering a collection of essays, books, articles, maps, and illustrations that provide insights into a variety of issues surrounding slavery in the United States: the slave trade, the abolitionist movement, the Slave Trade Acts, the campaign to revive the trade, and the end of African deportation.

The examples we used in this chapter focused on finding primary sources related to American history and culture. Content for British history and culture can be identified in the same way (see the appendix for examples). Primary sources are an essential component to research because they help bring the period you are studying to life and allow you to see how certain events or situations can influence an author and explain a theme in a literary work. Using primary sources develops your own interpretation of a work, which relying solely on secondary sources does not. Refer to your library's specialized **research guides** or your librarian for assistance if you are unable to find the primary resources you need.

7

Finding
Background Information

For some assignments, you will need to find background information about an author's life or about the time in which the author lived. For instance, you will write better about the decadence in *The Great Gatsby* if you understand a bit about American society after World War I and during Prohibition. Knowing that England was at war during nearly the entire time period in which Jane Austen set her novels will lead you to research topics you might not have initially thought of. Yet for some research assignments, your professor may ask you to leave out any biographical information about the author and focus instead on the author's work. So the need for personal background or historical context depends on your particular course and topic.

Most of the reference sources (e.g., encyclopedias, dictionaries) discussed in this chapter—both in print and online—offer brief, basic information, generally only a paragraph or two with an overview of an author's life, works, and sometimes the author's historical context. Most also list books and articles for further reading. A few of the resources in this chapter do offer more than the basics. For example, the several literary criticism series published by Gale offer full or excerpted essays on authors and their work that you may not have access to in an online library database. *Dictionary of Literary Biography* sometimes contains original essays on works and authors that are not to be found anywhere else.

You should be able to find some of this information on the Internet, so we discuss some resources there that may be of use to you if you decide to go that route. But a caveat: for general information that is easy to come by and regurgitate, Web sites of dubious credibility abound. Be careful as you wade through them. In the context of a college classroom and an academic research assignment, your professor will probably prefer that you use academic reference resources of the type that are available at your library.

Library Sources for Biographical and Historical Information

To find resources in your library with biographical and historical background information on your author, you will need to use your library databases (see chapters 2 and 3). The databases that a college or university library has access to will vary from place to place, so your library may not have access to all the ones discussed in this chapter. If your library does not have a database referenced in this chapter, there is a good chance that it has the print version. Your librarian will also be able to help you identify the databases or resources that your library does have access to and that will meet your need for this type of information.

One of the most common and useful resources for biographical information on an author is the *Dictionary of Literary Biography* (*DLB*). This resource is available as its own database (*DLB Complete Online*, see assets. cengage.com/pdf/fs_dlb-online.pdf), as a part of other database packages (e.g., *Literature Resource Center*), and in print. It provides both biographical and historical background on thousands of authors as well as original essays of literary criticism. Besides authors of novels, poetry, short stories, and plays, the *DLB* provides information on essayists, literary critics, historians, journalists, and biographers. Each volume of the print version, over four hundred in all, focuses on an author or group of authors. Examples are *Langston Hughes: A Documentary Volume*, *Modern Spanish-American Poets*, *British Novelists between the Wars*, *American Short Story Writers since World War II*, and *Victorian Women Poets*. The online version contains over sixteen thousand entries, including thousands of images, and allows you to search for them by keyword and author name (see chapter 3 on how to use *Literature Resource Center*, which includes the *DLB*).

Other resources for biographical information focus on authors of a specific nationality. *Oxford Dictionary of National Biography* (*Oxford DNB*, www.oxforddnb.com) provides entries for major British figures from the fourth century BCE to the twenty-first century. The length and depth of each dictionary article vary depending on the figure: the entry for Shakespeare is forty-nine pages in the print version, Austen's is eighteen pages, and Mary Jane Seacole—one of the few black women to write about her experience of the white, male-dominated world of the nineteenth-century British Empire—gets about a page. You can expect to find at least something about most British authors in this database, no matter how little known, because of its expansive historical scope.

The main search box for the online database version searches only the dictionary article titles. If your paper is on a work by Shakespeare and you need background information about him, enter his name in the main search field, and you will receive results for both articles and images (fig. 40). The advanced search options are available on the left-hand side of the results screen under "Modify Search," or by choosing

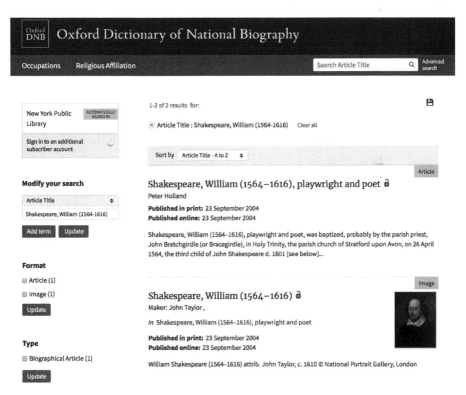

Fig. 40. Using the *Oxford Dictionary of National Biography* online interface to search for *William Shakespeare*

"Advanced Search" from the home page. These advanced options allow you to narrow the more than 75,000 articles in various ways, including by format (article, image, or audio), date, location, whether or not the article contains an image, author's occupation, author's religion, author's sex, and more. The advanced search also gives you the option to search for your keywords within various different fields, including article title, image caption, and full text.

The print version of the *Oxford DNB* contains the same content as the database, for the most part, and is organized alphabetically by last name into sixty volumes. There has been disagreement among scholars about the credibility of some of the information in this resource. Think back to our discussion of credibility and the need for evaluation in chapter 4: that need applies not only to information you find on the Internet but indeed to any source of information you use for research. At the time that this dictionary was published, there was "controversy and discussion" about the "accuracy of some of the information, authorship of entries, and similar issues" (Baker and Huling 61). The online version is continually updated, however, and errors have been corrected. If you use the print version, check its information against a second source. It is a good idea to do such checking no matter what source you are using, because even the most scholarly and authoritative one can contain mistakes.

The *American National Biography* (*ANB*, www.anb.org/aboutanb .html) focuses on American figures of note and provides biographical "portraits of more than 19,000 men and women—from all eras and walks of life—whose lives have shaped the nation." The online version of this resource (www.anb.org) is updated semiannually to revise current entries and add new ones, so if your library has this database, it will include many modern American authors. (The print version, published in 1999, does not.) The interface offers a "Quick Search" option where you can simply search for your author's name. If you are doing a research paper on *The Great Gatsby* and want to research the life of F. Scott Fitzgerald, enter his name in the "Search by Name" field, and you will receive one result. If you are conducting a broader search or would like to browse a list of authors in a certain category, you can use the many other options available on the advanced search form. To browse a list of African American authors, for instance, you can choose "Black History" from the "Special Collection" options and select the "Writing and Publishing" occupation. This search results in ninety-six entries including authors such as James Baldwin and Gwendolyn Brooks (fig. 41).

Another worthwhile biographical database is *Biography Reference Center*, which provides over 430,000 biographical entries for notable figures from all over the world, both historical and modern. It also contains the full contents of other databases, like *American National Biography*. It is not literary-specific, but you are able to search the database by name, occupation, country, nationality, and more. Browsing the database by genre allows you to narrow your search universe to authors and further narrow that to type of author.

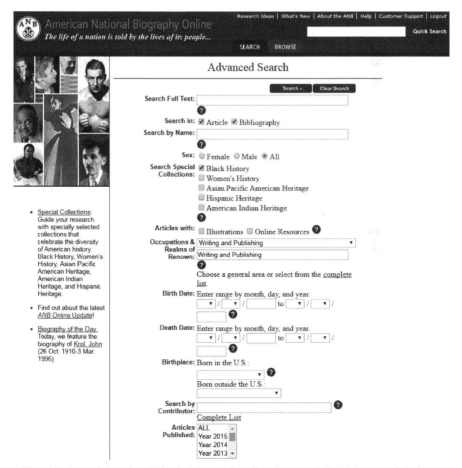

Fig. 41. Searching for "Black History" collection and "Writing and Publishing" occupation

In addition to databases, there are many print resources, which your library probably has, that contain helpful background information. How you are able to search for and locate these resources will depend on what information is available in your library's discovery system or catalog. Some systems will allow you to search only certain pieces of information, such as title, author, and Library of Congress subject headings (see chapter 2 for information about them); others will allow you to search the table of contents or even the full text of some books. If, for example, you are writing a paper on a work by Baldwin, you can search for his name in your library database or, to get more results, use a broader term, such as *African American authors*, *American authors* AND *social criticism*, *American authors* AND *race*, or simply *American authors*. Searching for *James Baldwin* in the Western Oregon University library discovery system gives 323 results. If we limit the physical location to "Reference," the results are 22. Among them are print versions of the resources we have already discussed in this chapter, but there are also titles like the *Encyclopedia of Literature and Politics: Censorship, Revolution, and Writing*, edited by M. Keith Booker, and *The Oxford Encyclopedia of American Literature*, edited by Jay Parini (fig. 42).

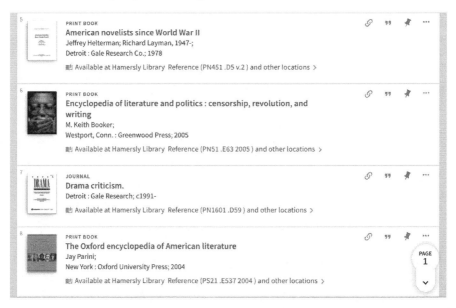

Fig. 42. Limiting the *James Baldwin* search with "Reference"

See the appendix to this volume for a list of common print reference sources that contain background information. If any of the books listed there sound relevant to your research, try searching for them in your library database by title. It is a good idea to try multiple approaches to searching for these types of resources, because they are sometimes no longer kept in the reference collection—most libraries have shrunk their reference collections but may still have the books in the general collection. Certain resources will not come up in a search by keyword or author name because they are too old for their full contents to be indexed in the database. To find such resources, you need to know that they exist and search for them by title.

Internet Sources for Biographical and Historical Information

Wikipedia can be a good source of general background information, as this is what encyclopedias are for. It can be particularly helpful, when you are writing a research paper and need more than just cursory information, to go directly to the Web sites, articles, or books cited at the bottom of the *Wikipedia* article as the sources for its information. For all Web sites you use, whether they come from *Wikipedia* or from this book, you must evaluate the credibility of the information they present (see chapter 4 on evaluating Web sites). This chapter and the appendix give you examples of Web sites to consider consulting, but we cannot be comprehensive, and their presence in this book does not mean that your professor will approve of your using them.

A major resource available on the Internet that often goes untapped is a type of library-created Web page called a research guide. Most college and university libraries maintain research guides for literature students (and for students in all subjects of study). Librarians create these guides, which contain a plethora of information on databases, library resources, and Web sites, as well as guidance on conducting research and using the information you find in your research assignments (figs. 43 and 44). These guides, from your own library and other college and university libraries across the country, can be valuable when you are doing research on the Internet. Keep in mind that some of the resources on such a guide (e.g., the books in the library's collection) will be available only to students of a specific college or university, so it makes sense to search your own library's Web site for such a literature research guide before you consider guides from other libraries (fig. 45).

If your library does not have research guides, or you want to browse the resources that other libraries link to, the easiest way to search for these guides is to enter your keywords (e.g., *English literature* or *women writers*) plus the keywords *research guides* or *libguides* into an Internet search engine. *LibGuides* is the name of the tool that many academic libraries use to create these guides, so the URLs typically contain the word "libguides." You can also search the library Web site for a specific college or university and look for the phrase "research guides," often found under headings like "help," "research support," "research help," and so on (fig. 46).

Fig. 43. American literature research guide for *UW Libraries*

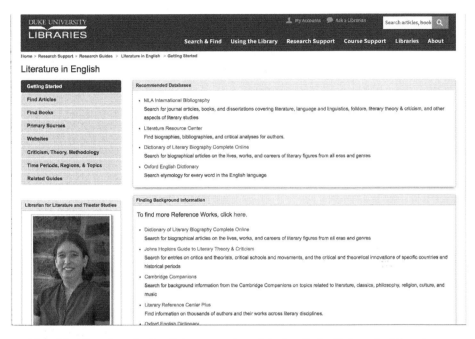

Fig. 44. Literature in English research guide for *Duke University Libraries*

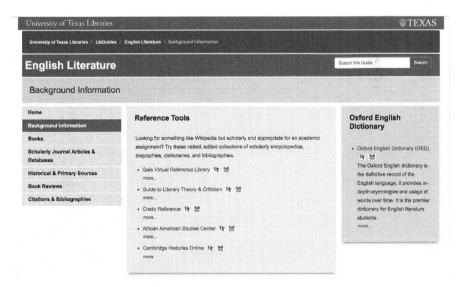

Fig. 45. English literature research guide for *University of Texas Libraries*

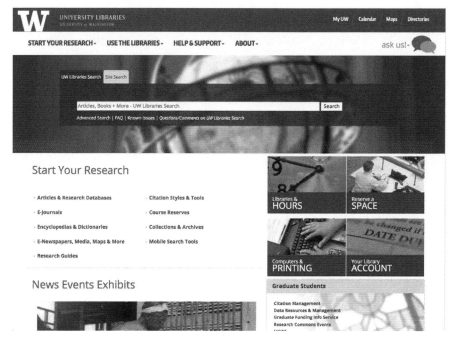

Fig. 46. "Research Guides" at *UW Libraries*

Example Internet Resources

Luminarium: Anthology of English Literature (luminarium.org)

A site created and maintained by one person, Anniina Jokinen, but with material sourced from *The Norton Anthology of English Literature*, *The Encyclopædia Britannica*, and *The Cambridge Guide to Literature in English*, among others. It is organized by literary period but can also be navigated by clicking on an author's name in the list of authors near the bottom of the page. The entry for each author includes a list of works, a biography, criticism, quotations, and sometimes more. The authors included in the site are limited to those in the traditional literary canon.

Literary Resources on the Net (andromeda.rutgers.edu/~jlynch/Lit/)

A directory of Web sites with information about English and American authors, literature, and literary criticism, curated by Jack Lynch, a professor at Rutgers University. It is entirely made up of links to other Web sites, which need to be evaluated on their own credentials. Navigate it by clicking on the relevant time period or genre. For example, if you are writing a research paper on a work by one of the Brontë sisters, you could choose either the "Victorian" category or the "Women's Literature and Feminism" category—both will bring you to pages in the directory that list links to Web sites with information about these authors.

Perspectives in American Literature (www.paulreuben.website)

A Web site that provides biographical information on American authors as well as lists of sources for literary criticism and bibliographies. The author entries can be navigated by time period—called "Chapters" on the site (e.g., "Early American Lit 1700–1800," "The Harlem Renaissance")—or alphabetically by author last name using the "Alphabetical List" at the top of the page. The entries vary greatly in length and depth: some are simply links to other sites and a bibliography of works; others contain extensive biographies, chronologies, lists of awards, as well as bibliographies and links to outside sources. The site is created and maintained by Paul Reuben, a professor emeritus from California State University, Stanislaus.

Literary Criticism Collection (ipl.org/div/litcrit/)

A partnership between the Internet Public Library and several universities across the country, this is a curated collection of Web sites with critical and biographical information about authors and their literary works. It is no longer being updated and so does not contain information on new authors, but what it does contain on British and American authors from the past should still be relevant to your research. You can browse the list of sites by author last name, title of work, nationality of author, or literary period. If you want to find biographical or contextual historical information about an author, such as F. Scott Fitzgerald, click the "E–F" link under "Browse for Criticism by Author's Last Name," then navigate to "Fitzgerald, F. Scott (1896–1940)," where you will see links to several biographical sites and sites with other types of information.

Voices from the Gaps (hdl.handle.net/11299/164018)

A Web site created by Toni McNaron and Carol Miller, professors at the University of Minnesota, to "uncover, highlight, and share the works of marginalized artists, predominately women writers of color living and working in North America." It is now in the university's digital archive and can be navigated by searching for an author's name, the title of her work, time period, or ethnicity. The collection can also be browsed by title, subject, or more specific categories. Author entries include a biography and bibliography.

Finding a Definition or the Source of a Quotation

Other types of background information you could need for research assignments are word definitions and author quotations. Although there are many Web sites that provide definitions, if you are looking for a literary term or movement, the quick definitions you find online will not be as helpful as those you will find in the resources described in this book. In addition to the reference sources already described, your library will have a collection of various types of dictionaries—ask a librarian or search your library database for *dictionary, unabridged dictionary, abridged dictionary,* or *literary dictionary* to find them.

When you study literature from the past, you will find that some words had different meanings, connotations, and associations when the author wrote them than they do now. When you run across such a word, you will need a historical dictionary, like the *Oxford English Dictionary* (*OED*). Most libraries subscribe to the *OED* online or have it in print. Each entry in the *OED* contains information on the origin and history of the word, including the date of the first recorded use of the word, variant spellings and pronunciations, and the ways that the meaning and usage of the word have changed over time. For example, the entry for *girl* in the *OED* online tells us that this word historically has meant "a child of either sex; a young person" (fig. 47). Underneath this definition are several chronologically organized sample texts that use the word in this way. One is from the *Canterbury Tales*, when Chaucer talks about "yonge gerles of the diocise" ("young girls of the diocese"). This usage of *girl* went out of fashion after the fifteenth century, so we would misunderstand this line from Chaucer's Prologue if we did not know the definition of the word during his time.

Searching for the source of a quotation is tricky in today's online world. Quotations on the Internet are one of the most unreliable categories of information. They are so often misattributed that it seems there are nearly as many Web sites devoted to debunking such mistakes (fig. 48). For this reason, we urge you to use library resources to track down a quotation.

Several databases mentioned in this chapter and in the appendix— *Literary Reference Center, Poetry and Short Story Reference Center,* and *Literature Resource Center*—include the full text of many primary literary sources that can be searched using keywords from the quotation you are seeking. Additional databases and Web sites for finding searchable

Fig. 47. Definition of *girl* at *OED*

Fig. 48. Web page that debunks misattributed quotations

primary sources can be found in chapter 6. The library also has print resources that can help you locate a quotation. One is a concordance. Concordances generally exist only for authors who are in the literary canon, like Shakespeare, William Wordsworth, D. H. Lawrence, John Keats, Edgar Allan Poe, and Emily Dickinson. A concordance can help if you remember that a line from a Dickinson poem has something to do with a star but cannot place the poem. Instead of having to thumb through the entire body of her poetry looking for "star," you can turn to the S section of a concordance of her work (Rosenbaum 710). There you will find a list of lines from her poems that contain the word, and for each of these lines you are given the first line of the poem (since most of Dickinson's poems do not have titles), the poem number, and the line number (fig. 49). To learn if your library has a concordance for the author you are studying, conduct a keyword search using your library's database or catalog for your author's last name and *concordance*.

STAR (CONTINUED)	FIRST LINE	POEM	LINE
OR VIOLATE A STAR—	WHAT SOFT—CHERUBIC	401	4
A STAR—NOT FAR ENOUGH TO SEEK— : : : :	A MURMUR IN THE TREES--	416	3
OR STAR—COME OUT—WITHIN—	WE GROW ACCUSTOMED TO	419	12
AS SUNS—DISSOLVE [ANNUL] A STAR— . . .	NO CROWD THAT HAS	515	12
THEN—PROMPTER THAN [PUNCTUAL AS] A STAR .	I LIKE TO SEE IT LAP	585	15
WITH BUT A SINGLE STAR—	THE NIGHT WAS WIDE, AND	589	2
AND EASY AS A STAR	THEY SHUT ME UP IN PROSE	613	10
WITHDREW THE FURTHEST STAR	I COULD SUFFICE FOR HIM,	643	10
AS ONE SHOULD SUE A STAR—	THE HEAVEN VESTS FOR	694	10
AND YET THE NEWEST STAR—	THE DAY UNDRESSED—	716	6
BUT THE REMOTEST STAR—	THE MOON WAS BUT A CHIN	737	14
AND WITHHOLD A STAR—	ALL I MAY, IF SMALL,	819	6
AND IN THE NORTH, THE STAR—	THESE ARE THE SIGNS TO	1077	12
AT NIGHT BENEATH [BELOW] THE STAR . . .	THE SNOW THAT NEVER	1133	6
THE ROAD WAS LIT WITH [BY] MOON AND STAR— .	THE ROAD WAS LIT WITH	1450	1
AS GRAPHIC AS A STAR	WHOEVER DISENCHANTS	1451	6
WITHIN [IN / TO] A STAR—	HE LIVED THE LIFE OF	1525	8
ACCOMPANIES A STAR.	NO MATTER WHERE THE	1541	4
IS VALID AS A STAR—	TO HER DERIDED HOME	1586 V	
SECRETED IN A STAR.	WHO ABDICATED AMBUSH	1616	8
LIGHTLY STEPPED A YELLOW STAR	LIGHTLY STEPPED A YELLOW	1672	1
AND PRANKS THE NORTHERN STAR	THESE ARE THE DAYS THAT	1696	2

Fig. 49. Instances of *star* from a concordance of Emily Dickinson's poems

If you are searching for a quotation that is well known, you may be able to find its author in a quotation dictionary. Some quotation dictionaries are available online, such as the *Oxford Dictionary of Quotations*, which is part of *Oxford Reference Online*. Your library will also likely have several print quotation dictionaries, which you can find by searching for *quotation dictionary* in your library database or catalog. These dictionaries tend to be organized alphabetically by subject (beauty, love, poetry). They also have an index at the back. Every quotation dictionary will contain a different set of quotations.

Works Cited

Baker, Nancy L., and Nancy Huling. *A Research Guide for Undergraduate Students: English and American Literature.* 6th ed., Modern Language Association of America, 2006.

Rosenbaum, Stanford Patrick, editor. *A Concordance to the Poems of Emily Dickinson.* Cornell UP, 1964.

8

Managing Sources and Creating Your Bibliography

Your professor will expect you to document in a consistent way all the works you make use of in your paper. Most likely you will be asked to use an accepted citation style—in your literature classes this will usually be MLA style. You should cite any work you **summarize** or **paraphrase**, works you quote, and works whose ideas you use to build your argument or formulate your own interpretation. Your **in-text citation** will consist of parenthetical references or notes, where appropriate (fig. 50). You will also need to create a works-cited list: you indicate in the text of your paper the instances in which you are making reference, summarizing, paraphrasing, or quoting, then give full publication information for those works that you cite—usually at the end of a paper, but sometimes in footnotes or endnotes, depending on the citation style (fig. 51).

Citing your sources in a research paper is not simply about giving credit to the work of other people that you used, avoiding accusations of **plagiarism**. This is one reason to cite sources, but there are others. Scholarship, which is what you are practicing when you write a research paper, is a conversation among people trying to build knowledge in a certain field. None of the knowledge that has resulted from research—be it in literature, psychology, or biology—came from individuals working in a vacuum, it came from scholars engaging with one another and exchanging different perspectives, interpretations, and data. Scholars must know who said what, who agreed with whom, and who challenged whom. They must also be able to evaluate the strength of the evidence behind a conclusion and know where they can go to learn more. This type of community can exist only if scholars acknowledge in their work

MLA:

We can deduce that the future Lady Bertram was beautiful as a young woman from the information that some of the family's "acquaintance" consider the two younger sisters "quite as handsome as Miss Maria" (Austen 5).

APA:

We can deduce that the future Lady Bertram was beautiful as a young woman from the information that some of the family's "acquaintance" consider the two younger sisters "quite as handsome as Miss Maria" (Austen, 1814, 5).

Chicago Author-Date References:

We can deduce that the future Lady Bertram was beautiful as a young woman from the information that some of the family's "acquaintance" consider the two younger sisters "quite as handsome as Miss Maria" (Austen 1814).

Chicago Footnotes/Endnotes:

We can deduce that the future Lady Bertram was beautiful as a young woman from the information that some of the family's "acquaintance" consider the two younger sisters "quite as handsome as Miss Maria."[1]

Fig. 50. Comparing styles for in-text citation

which other scholars they read, referred to, and engaged with. Citing sources demonstrates your understanding of, and engagement with, the scholarly conversation about your topic.

Creating In-Text Citations and a Works-Cited List

Scholars in the same field can better engage with one another's work if they format their in-text citations and bibliographies in the same way. The position of a comma or issue number of a journal may seem unimportant, but having formatting standards promotes better and more efficient communication among scholars.

Works Cited

Austen, Jane. *Mansfield Park*. Edited by Kathryn Sutherland, Penguin Books, 2014.

---. "To Cassandra Austen." *Jane Austen's Letters*, edited by Deirdre Le Faye, 3rd ed., Oxford

UP, 1995, pp. 25-28.

Brophy, Elizabeth Bergen. *Women's Lives and the Eighteenth-Century English Novel*. U of South

Florida P, 1991.

Copeland, Edward. "Money." *The Cambridge Companion to Jane Austen*, edited by Copeland

and Juliet McMaster, Cambridge UP, 1997, pp. 131-48.

Green, Katherine Sobba. *The Courtship Novel 1740-1820: A Feminized Genre*. UP of Kentucky,

1991.

"Heavy, *Adj.^{1}* and *N.*" *Oxford English Dictionary*, Oxford UP, 2015,

www.oed.com/view/Entry/85246?rskey=aIe8OM&result=1.

Hinnant, Charles H. "Jane Austen's 'Wild Imagination': Romance and the Courtship Plot in the

Six Canonical Novels." *Narrative*, vol. 14, no. 3, 2006, pp. 294-310. *JSTOR*,

www.jstor.org/stable/20107392.

Johnson, Claudia L. "*Mansfield Park*: Confusions of Guilt and Revolutions of Mind." *Mansfield

Park*, by Jane Austen, edited by Johnson, W. W. Norton, 1998, pp. 458-76.

Tomalin, Claire. *Jane Austen: A Life*. Vintage, 1999.

Fig. 51. Example of MLA works-cited-list entries

MLA Style

In the fields of language and literature and in writing courses, the most commonly used formatting and citation style is published by the Modern Language Association (MLA). The 2016 eighth edition of the *MLA Handbook* and its free online companion site (style.mla.org) are your best sources for information about MLA style. Your library probably has several copies of the handbook, but often it is considered reference material and therefore may be available for use only inside the library. If you will be writing many literary research papers, you may want to obtain your own copy or the e-book version of the handbook.

MLA style uses brief parenthetical in-text citations throughout the body of a paper that key to an alphabetized bibliographic list called "Works Cited" at the end of the paper. For example, imagine that you are writing a paper discussing the use of fairy tales in literature and want to use information from the book *The Burning of Bridget Cleary*, by Angela Bourke. The in-text citation will look like this:

> Folk tales about fairies served numerous purposes, including instructing children about good behavior (Bourke 41).

The parenthetical "Bourke 41" tells your reader that you are paraphrasing material from page 41 of a work by an author whose last name is Bourke. The works-cited-list entry for Bourke reads:

> Bourke, Angela. *The Burning of Bridget Cleary*. Viking, 1999.

Readers see when the work was written and have the information they need to search for it. Once the book is in hand, they can turn to page 41 to read the discussion that you paraphrased in your paper and, if they choose, learn more about what Bourke has to say on the subject.

In the eighth edition of the *MLA Handbook*, works-cited-list entries are structured according to a template of core elements (fig. 52). As the MLA explains, the core elements are "facts common to most works" (3). The terms on the template stand in for a range of publication details. For example, the publisher might be the company that produced a book or the arts organization that staged a play. The "Title of Source" element can be used to provide a published title (like *The Burning of Bridget Cleary*) or a description of an untitled work (like a letter). Omit any element other than "Title of Source" from your entry if it doesn't apply to the work you're citing. The template also tells you how to structure and punctuate your works-cited-list entry.

Fig. 52. Template of core elements in works-cited-list entry (*MLA Handbook,* 8th ed.)

APA and Chicago Styles

There are other citation and formatting styles that you may be asked to use, depending on your course and professor—for example, the styles published by the American Psychological Association (APA) and by the University of Chicago. Your library will also have copies of *The Chicago Manual of Style* and the *Publication Manual of the American Psychological Association,* since they are often used in other fields of study. On the question of which style to use, check your syllabus or ask your professor before you begin your paper.

Organizing Your Research

Having a plan for organizing your research before you begin will make creating your bibliography at the end easier and more efficient. It will also help you along the way as you write your paper. If you have a system, it will be much easier for you to locate the sources you obtained when you need to quote or summarize them or review a discussion or idea.

The many tools available to help you organize your sources and create your bibliography all have the same general functions. They will automatically format citations for you either from information you enter manually or that you export from a library discovery system or research databases like the ones discussed in chapter 3. They can often convert citations from one style to another, in the event you need to use a source in more than one course, each professor requiring a different citation style. Many research management and citation tools allow you to annotate your entries—what the source was about, what idea it sparked for you, and how you plan to use that idea in your paper. This feature can help later if you need to go back and revisit a source.

Some of these digital tools are expensive, complicated, and necessary only at an advanced level of scholarship; others are free, often unreliable, and choked by online advertisements. There are several that sit in the middle of the spectrum, however: tools that are free or low-cost to students (either through individual accounts or institutional subscriptions through your library), Web-based and therefore accessible from any device with Internet access, and easy to use. The following is not a comprehensive list of all such tools, but does represent some of the most common and easy-to-use of the current options.

Digital Research Management and Citation Tools

Zotero (zotero.org)

> ACCESS MODEL: free and **open-source**. The code for the tool is modifiable by users, and many developers have contributed code to update, change, and improve the product.

> BASIC FUNCTIONS: managing and organizing your research, creating citations in various styles (using entered information or information imported from databases or other citation management tools), filing and storing (you can save your research articles and chapters in the tool), and connecting and collaborating with other users

Mendeley (mendeley.com)

ACCESS MODEL: free to people who create an account

BASIC FUNCTIONS: managing and organizing your research, creating citations in various styles, social networking (you can connect and collaborate with other users), sharing your research sources with other users on this platform (i.e., they are publicly searchable)

RefWorks (refworks.com)

ACCESS MODEL: available to anyone whose institution subscribes and available to individuals on a thirty-day free trial basis

BASIC FUNCTIONS: managing and organizing your research, creating citations in various styles (using entered information or information imported from databases or other citation management tools), file sharing

EndNote (endnote.com)

ACCESS MODEL: available to anyone whose institution subscribes and available to individuals as a free, online-only account or with the purchase of the software

BASIC FUNCTIONS: managing and organizing your research, creating citations in various styles (using entered information or information imported from databases or other citation management tools), collaboration tools and file sharing, and filing and storing

EasyBib (easybib.com)

ACCESS MODEL: free account available with limited options and many ads; upgrading to an EasyBib Pro account gets rid of ads and provides more options

BASIC FUNCTIONS: organizing and managing your research, creating citations in various styles (only MLA, APA, and Chicago styles are available for free, other styles are available in the Pro account), and connecting and collaborating with other users. Searches the Internet for citation information (you often need only enter a URL or book title in order to create the citation).

NoodleTools (noodletools.com)

ACCESS MODEL: options for a free account, individual subscription, or institutional subscription

BASIC FUNCTIONS: with the free "MLA Lite" account, you can only create citations in MLA style. Both the individual and institutional subscriptions provide full access to all the basic and advanced functions that you would expect from such a platform, including organizing and managing your research, creating citations in various styles and switching between styles, and making a project public in order to collaborate with other users. There is some integration with *Google Docs*, and you can create to-do lists in projects.

Your library may already subscribe to a citation management tool and make accounts available to students through the library Web site. If it does, use that tool, it will be the one with which your librarians and IT staff members are the most familiar and can best help you. Your library may offer workshops on how to use the tool.

Work Cited

MLA Handbook. 8th ed., Modern Language Association of America, 2016.

9

Guides to Research in English and American Literature

There are occasions when investigating an author, creative work, or literary theme requires more specific types of information than those we have covered so far. What if you are writing an in-depth thesis on an author or work that has not been examined by scholars to date? What if you need to see the original manuscript of a novel that is not available online, or track down a source in which a writer published a poem for the first time? For such projects you must go beyond the basics of searching library databases, which have been the focus of this book. You will need specialized resources to get the information you need. If you don't know where to start, ask your librarian. Librarians are knowledgeable about the information landscapes of different disciplines. In this chapter, we look at a few resources that might help you pursue a more specialized research project within the discipline of literary studies.

Suppose you are studying a work of fiction by an eighteenth-century author and, uncertain about the use of particular words in the text, think it would be helpful to compare the original manuscript with the corresponding published text. How do you go about finding where the manuscript is located? How do you discover all the published versions of that text? Or suppose you are researching a nineteenth-century Australian bush poet and want to know where one of the poems was first published. How would you figure this out? Although the resources we have discussed in previous chapters are unlikely to help you with these types of questions, consulting a published research guide (different from the online library research guides discussed in chapter 7) is an excellent way to solve more complicated information needs. A research guide provides lists of and discusses specialized tools—bibliographies, indexes, databases, and catalogs. Some of those guides focus on resources for the study of English and American literature. We look at two, a book and a series of books, pointing out the features that make them essential for the serious literary scholar.

Harner's *Literary Research Guide*

Librarians and scholars who specialize in English and American literature often refer to James L. Harner's *Literary Research Guide: An Annotated Listing of Reference Sources in English Literary Studies* as the bible of literary research. If you are writing an in-depth paper for your class, planning to major in English and write a thesis, or considering getting an advanced degree in English, you should be aware of Harner. His guide covers the major research tools available for the study of literature: specialized dictionaries and encyclopedias; bibliographies; guides to manuscripts and archival collections, to primary works, to finding scholarship and criticism, to finding dissertations and theses; biographical sources, periodicals, and tools for finding resources by genre. It is organized by national literature: English, Irish, Scottish, Welsh, American, and other literatures in English. In these categories, resources are further broken down by time period or in other ways. For instance, the section "American Literature" includes regional literature, ethnic and minority literatures, African American literatures, and nineteenth- and twentieth-century literature.

The value of the *Literary Research Guide* is not just in its coverage of these resources but also in its ease of use. To return to the task of locating an eighteenth-century manuscript, in Harner we can go to the section "Restoration and Eighteenth-Century Literature," then to "Guides to Primary Works," then to "Manuscripts" (168–69). Listed are tools specifically designed to identify where manuscripts are located for this time period, such as the *Index of English Literary Manuscripts, 1700–1800.* Informative summaries of each resource give you an idea of what you can expect to find by using that particular tool. What about the first publication of the Australian poem? Under "Other Literatures in English" there is the section "Australian Literature." The category "Poetry:

Guides to Primary Works" gives a tool for identifying magazines and newspapers in existence in Australia before 1850 that published poetry (543–44).

Series on Literary Research from Scarecrow Press

But what if you need more resources to answer your questions? The books in the series Literary Research: Strategies and Sources, from Scarecrow Press, can be useful because they are designed to help scholars researching a particular literary period or national literature.

Scarecrow's series goes a step further than Harner in two ways: one, an entire volume, not just a section or chapter, is devoted to information

EBOOK
Literary research and Canadian literature strategies and sources
Gabriella Natasha Reznowski, 1974-
2011 Lanham, Md. : Scarecrow Press

Online access >

Send to ───────────────────────────────────

| E-MAIL | CITATION | PERMALINK | PRINT | REFWORKS | ENDNOTE | BIBTEX | EXPORT RIS |

View It ───────────────────────────────────

Current UW students, faculty, and staff   Log in for all services

Ebook Central Academic Complete   [view license terms]
Public notes:
   UW restricted

Item Details ───────────────────────────────────

Title	Literary research and Canadian literature strategies and sources
Author	Gabriella Natasha Reznowski, 1974- >
LCSH and PCI subjects	Canadian literature -- Research -- Methodology >
	Canadian literature -- Information resources >
Description	1. Basics of online searching -- 2. General literary reference sources -- 3. Library catalogs -- 4. Print and electronic bibliographies, indexes, and annual reviews -- 5. Scholarly journals -- 6. Periodicals,

Fig. 53. Gabriella Reznowski's *Literary Research and Canadian Literature*

on one literary period or national literature; two, each volume discusses research strategies for that period or literature. Whereas there are twenty-five pages devoted to Canadian literature in Harner, with one page on manuscript resources, in Gabriella Reznowski's *Literary Research and Canadian Literature Strategies and Sources* (2011), an entire chapter provides information on tools for identifying manuscripts and dealing with archival materials for Canadian authors (fig. 53).

Each volume in the Scarecrow series analyzes and compares both print and electronic sources. Chapters typically cover general literary reference materials, library catalogs, bibliographies, indexes, annual reviews, scholarly journals, contemporary reviews, period journals and newspapers, microform and digital collections, manuscripts and archives, and Internet resources. Currently there are thirteen volumes in the series:

Literary Research and the British Romantic Era, by Peggy Keeran and Jennifer Bowers, 2005.

Literary Research and the Era of American Nationalism and Romanticism, by Angela Courtney, 2008.

Literary Research and American Modernism, by Robert N. Matuozzi and Elizabeth B. Lindsay, 2008.

Literary Research and the American Realism and Naturalism Period, by Linda L. Stein and Peter J. Lehu, 2009.

Literary Research and Irish Literature, by J. Greg Matthews, 2009.

Literary Research and the Literatures of Australia and New Zealand, by H. Faye Christenberry and Angela Courtney, 2010.

Literary Research and British Modernism, by Alison M. Lewis, 2010.

Literary Research and the British Renaissance and Early Modern Period, by Jennifer Bowers and Peggy Keeran, 2010.

Literary Research and the Victorian and Edwardian Ages, 1830–1910, by Melissa S. Van Vuuren, 2011.

Literary Research and Canadian Literature, by Gabriella Natasha Reznowski, 2011.

Literary Research and Postcolonial Literatures in English, by H. Faye Christenberry et al., 2012.

Literary Research and the British Eighteenth Century, by Peggy Keeran and Jennifer Bowers, 2013.

Literary Research and British Postmodernism, by Bridgit McCafferty and Arianne Hartsell-Gundy, 2015.

You may have these books at your library. If not, you should be able to get them through the interlibrary loan system.

Most undergraduate course assignments require the identification of just a few secondary resources to support an argument or thesis, so it is unlikely that you will need to consult the research guides described in this chapter. But if you want to know more about an author, creative work, or literary topic that means going beyond the steps of searching standard databases, keep these resources in mind.

Selective Bibliography of Sources for English and American Literature

Subject-Specific and Interdisciplinary Databases

Academic Search. EBSCO.

> Covers all subject areas and includes both scholarly journals and popular magazines, as well as a small selection of newspapers. There are almost 6,600 active full-text periodicals in the database, 6,000 of them peer-reviewed. Because this database provides the full text of a variety of resources, it is useful for identifying book reviews, performance reviews, and scholarly articles.

Annual Bibliography of English Language and Literature (ABELL). Modern Humanities Research Association, 1921–. Print and online.

> An important index to scholarly criticism on all areas of English literature, American literature, and other literatures written in English. The online version of *ABELL* makes it easy to locate citations of journal articles, book chapters, and book reviews from 1892 to the present. Subject areas covered are English language studies, bibliography studies (manuscript studies, textual studies, and the history of publishing), and cultural studies (custom, belief, narrative, song, dance, and material culture).

Expanded Academic Index ASAP. Gale/Cengage.

> Covers everything from art and literature to economics and the hard sciences. It includes the full text of some 2,800 popular and scholarly publications from across all subjects and disciplines, providing indexing for more than 5,000 periodicals.

FIAF International Index to Film Periodicals (FIAF). ProQuest.

> An essential resource for anyone interested in film studies, it contains over 500,000 article citations from more than 345 cinema and media-related journals and magazines. Offers in-depth coverage of film history, theory, and criticism from important academic and popular film sources. In addition to scholarly criticism, *FIAF* includes film reviews and interviews with directors and other important film industry figures.

Historical Abstracts and *America: History and Life*. EBSCO.

> Two essential resources for searching for scholarly information on the study of history. *Historical Abstracts* covers the history of the world excluding the United States and Canada, from the fifteenth century to the present. Content indexed in the database: scholarly articles, book reviews, and media reviews from 2,300 journals in over forty languages, from 1953 on. Books and book chapters are also indexed in *Historical Abstracts*. *America: History and Life* is the counterpart to *Historical Abstracts*, indexing over 1,800 journals from 1895 to the present that focus on American and Canadian history.

Humanities International Complete. EBSCO.

> Covers journals, books, and other important reference sources in the humanities. Provides full-text content for over 920 active journals and magazines and includes citations and abstracts for many more articles, essays, and reviews, as well as original creative works (e.g., poems, fiction, photographs, paintings, illustrations).

JSTOR. ITHAKA.

> Provides access to the full text of more than 10 million academic journal articles and books in seventy-five disciplines. Core scholarly journals and books in the humanities, social sciences, and sciences are in *JSTOR*. Check your library's subscription options to see if books are included.

Literature Online (LION). ProQuest.

> Unique among literary databases because it contains the full text of over 355,000 creative works, with scholarly criticism and reference resources. A selection of poetry, prose, and drama from the Anglo-Saxon period to the twentieth century and the full text of more than 400 scholarly journals and excerpts from literary encyclopedias,

bibliographies, and author biographies. Also there are video and audio clips of poets reading their poetry. If your library subscribes, the *Annual Bibliography of English Language and Literature* is incorporated into *LION* so you can search it to identify criticism on a particular author or work.

Literature Resource Center. Gale/Cengage.

Covers literary criticism, book reviews, and biographical sketches on more than 130,000 writers around the world from all time periods. Some 850,000 full-text articles, essays, and reviews from 390 journals and magazines are available.

MLA International Bibliography. Modern Language Association / EBSCO.

The leading resource for scholars and students of literary studies, language studies, linguistics, and folklore, covering content from more than 4,400 periodicals dating back as far as 1881 and including book chapters and monographs from over a thousand publishers. Doctoral dissertations and scholarly Web sites are also indexed. As of summer 2018, EBSCO offers a full-text version of the *MLA International Bibliography.* Full text of more than a thousand journals is available on this platform.

Project MUSE. Johns Hopkins UP.

A leading provider of digital scholarly content for the areas of the humanities and social sciences, containing complete, full-text versions of scholarly journals from more than 120 of the world's leading university presses and scholarly societies. Book collections on *Project MUSE* became available for the first time in 2012. Users can search fully integrated versions of book content along with scholarly journal content.

ProQuest Research Library. ProQuest.

A multidisciplinary database that contains a mix of scholarly journals, trade publications, popular magazines, and other sources across all subject areas, containing more than 6,000 periodical titles, most of which are available in full text. Because this database provides the full-text content of a variety of resources, it is useful for identifying book and performance reviews as well as research articles on a given topic.

World Wide Web

Google Scholar. Google.

> Provides an easy and quick way to search for scholarly literature across many disciplines and sources, with content from academic publishers, professional societies, online repositories, and universities. The full text of scholarly articles and books is not available for free; you can access it through your library's subscription.

Wikipedia: The Free Encyclopedia. Wikimedia Foundation.

> A free, crowd-sourced encyclopedia that is useful for finding background and overview information about nearly any topic. Critical, in-depth sources are often cited at the bottom of an article.

Book, Film, and Performance Reviews

Access World News. NewsBank.

> Provides full text of local, regional, national, and international newspapers from the 1980s to present, with content from over 10,000 sources, mostly but not all in English. Because newspapers often feature book, film, and performance reviews, they can be a good source for identifying reviews.

Book Review Index. Wilson, 1965–. Gale/Cengage. Print and online.

> Provides access to reviews of book and electronic media from more than 400 journals, general interest magazines, and newspapers. Online searching of the *Book Review Index Plus* is much easier than using the print index, as you can search by author, date, illustrator, review length, review source, reviewer, title, and title of review.

Combined Retrospective Index to Book Reviews in Humanities Journals, 1802–1974. Research Publications, 1982–84. Print.

> A core tool for identifying older book reviews in approximately 150 philosophy, classics, folklore, linguistics, music, and literature journals. The multivolume set is organized alphabetically by author or editor, then by book title.

Film Literature Index. Filmdex, 1973–. Indiana UP, 1976–2001. Print and online.

> Available in print from 1973 on and online from 1976 to 2001, an important source for locating film, television, video reviews, and articles from approximately 300 popular magazines and scholarly periodicals. In the print version, each volume covers a particular time period and is divided into two sections: film; television and video. The online version is free (webapp1.dlib.indiana.edu/fli/index.jsp).

Film Review Index. Oryx, 1986. Print.

> Two volumes that list articles and books on film from 1882 to 1985, with citations to film reviews, histories, and criticism for over seven thousand films.

Index to Book Reviews in the Humanities. 30 vols. Thomson, 1960–90. Print.

> An annual index to reviews in 676 scholarly journals devoted to literature, language, philosophy, the arts, travel, biography, classics, and folklore. Reviews are arranged by author name or, if the author is unknown, title of work.

NexisUni. Lexis/Nexis.

> Provides full-text access to world newspapers, mostly those published in English, from 1980 to the present and to law reviews and company information. For reviews of books, plays, or films, begin your search under the "News" option.

Times Literary Supplement Index. Newspaper Archive Developments, 1902–80. Print. *Times Literary Supplement Historical Archive.* Gale/Cengage, 1902–2011. Online.

> A valuable source of book reviews going back to the early twentieth century. The print index allows you to search in a selected time period. The electronic *Historical Archive* is easy to use and has newer content, added on a regular basis, and the full text of the reviews.

Primary Sources

Periodicals

American Periodicals Series Online. ProQuest.

A digitized collection of over 1,100 American magazines and journals that originated between 1740 and 1940. Some titles are covered into the twentieth century. You can limit your search to a particular magazine title or several aspects of information, such as an obituary, poem, illustration, or book review.

America's Historical Newspapers. NewsBank.

Has a number of modules to which libraries can subscribe, but the core resource is Early American Newspapers, 1690–1922. (Among the modules are African American Newspapers, 1827–1998; Hispanic American Newspapers, 1808–1980; Ethnic American Newspapers from the Balch Collection, 1799–1971; and the Washington Evening Star [1852–1981]). Offers digital facsimiles of thousands of titles from all fifty states.

British Periodicals. ProQuest.

Provides facsimile page images and searchable full text for almost 500 British periodicals published from the seventeenth century to the early twenty-first. Advanced search options make it easy to look for book reviews, poems, obituaries, advertisements, and other types of publications.

Humanities and Social Sciences Index Retrospective, 1907–84. Wilson.

An index to a wide range of important periodicals in the humanities and social sciences, covering 1,200 publications, mostly from the United States and the United Kingdom, including book reviews and articles from scholarly journals and popular magazines.

London Times Digital Archive (1785–2011). Gale/Cengage.

A full-text facsimile of more than 200 years of one of the most important newspapers in the world. Users can browse by date or use an advanced search to look for articles by author or subject or look only at obituaries, political news, editorials, or advertisements.

Poole's Index to Periodical Literature, 1802–81; supplements 1882–1906. Houghton, 1802–1906. Print.

> An important source for identifying articles in periodicals from the nineteenth century. You can look for information by author, title, or subject. Book reviews are also indexed.

ProQuest Historical Newspapers: New York Times (1851–2014). ProQuest.

> Offers full access to a major American newspaper. Users can scan through digitized news articles, photographs, advertisements, classified ads, obituaries, cartoons, and more. Searches may be limited to a date, date range, or topic. An advanced search screen allows you to find articles written by a particular author.

Reader's Guide Retrospective, 1890–1982. Wilson.

> The perfect tool for researching topics or events covered in the popular press. Covers about 550 magazines, mostly published in the United States—including *Harper's*, *Atlantic Monthly*, *The New Yorker*, and *Newsweek*. You can search by author, journal or magazine title, or subject, limiting results to a date, date range, or type of resource (article, book review, poem, or short story).

17th and 18th Century Burney Newspapers Collection. Gale/Cengage.

> The largest online collection of seventeenth- and eighteenth-century English news sources available—over a thousand pamphlets, proclamations, newsbooks, and newspapers from the period.

Wellesley Index to Victorian Periodicals (1824–1900). ProQuest.

> An important index to nineteenth-century articles that gives information on the author or contributor. Forty-five monthly and quarterly titles, from the beginning of the *Westminster Review*. Poetry is not indexed.

Books

Early American Imprints: Series I: Evans, 1639-1800. Readex.

> Includes every known book, pamphlet, and broadside published in America between 1640 and the first two decades of the nineteenth century, about 75,000 items. Users can browse by genre, subject,

author, history of printing, place of publication, and language. Among the searchable topics are agriculture, capital punishment, diseases, education, foreign affairs, medicine, religious thought, slavery, suffrage, and witchcraft.

Early English Books Online (EEBO). ProQuest.

Contains digital reproductions of virtually every work printed in England, Ireland, Scotland, Wales, and British North America from 1473 to 1700, from the first book published in English through the age of Spenser and Shakespeare, covering more than 130,000 titles and offering more than 17 million scanned pages of rare books and pamphlets.

Eighteenth Century Collections Online (ECCO). Gale/Cengage.

Has digitized over 200,000 volumes published in the United Kingdom during the eighteenth century—books, pamphlets, essays, broadsides, and more. Most of (but not all) the content is in English, and it may be searched by author, title, subject, or keyword. You can browse by eight different subject categories: history and geography; social sciences; religion and philosophy; general reference; fine arts; literature and language; law; and medicine, science, and technology.

Project Gutenberg (www.gutenberg.org).

Offers over 57,000 free e-books to download or read online. Many of the world's great literary classics are available, with a focus on older works that are no longer in copyright.

Online Digital Collections and Archives

British Library Digital Collections.

For free access to primary sources on British history and culture, no site equals the collections at the British Library. The library provides a browsable subject list of all the collections available. Of interest to those doing literary research is *Literature and Drama*, a collection of archives of postwar novelists and poets, literary organizations, theatrical archives and manuscripts, audiovisual recordings of drama and poetry in performance, collections of early English plays, and more.

British National Archives.

> Contains archival material essential to the study of British history. Some of the documents available to view for free are birth, marriage, and death records; census data; maps; information about soldiers in the First and Second World Wars; and more.

Library of Congress Digital Collections.

> The Library of Congress is the leader in digitizing primary sources on United States history and culture. There are 94 collections on United States history alone. Included in these collections are scans of historical documents, audio and video clips, interviews, photographs, and other primary source materials.

New York Public Library Digital Collections.

> The New York Public Library has digitized over 726,000 items. Included in its collections are photographs, maps, historical documents, sound recordings, and oral histories. You can search for a topic or browse by item, collection, or division.

Background Information on Authors, Literary Works, and Historical Time Periods

American Authors (public.wsu.edu/~campbelld/amlit/aufram.html)

> A list of American authors, mainly from the nineteenth century, with entries that link to information about their lives, works, and literary criticism of those works.

American National Biography. Oxford UP, 1920–2007. Print and online.

> Provides portraits of more than 19,000 men and women who shaped the nation, from all periods of American history, with overviews of literary works, biographical details, and location of key archival and manuscript collections.

Biography Reference Center. EBSCO.

> Provides over 430,000 biographical entries for notable figures from all over the world, both historical and contemporary, and the full

contents of key databases and series, like the *American National Biography*. It is not literary-specific, but searches can be limited by name, occupation, country, and nationality.

Cambridge Companions series. Cambridge UP. Print and online.

A series of guides that contain introductions to major authors as well as to broad literary periods, topics, and movements. One is the *Cambridge Companion to the Victorian Novel*. These companions are useful not only for finding background information on an author or historical time period but also for familiarizing readers with the scholarly conversation happening around an author or period. Each companion has a useful bibliography at the end.

Contemporary Authors. Gale/Cengage. Print and online.

Biographical database on more than 120,000 modern authors, from J. K. Rowling to Louise Erdrich to John Grisham. Each entry gives biographical data, a comprehensive list of published works, and a bibliography of books, magazines, and online articles that have been written about the author—in both newspapers and academic journals. It is updated annually and can be searched by name, title of work, subject or genre, nationality, date and place of birth, honors, and awards. The print version has the same content as the database but is organized alphabetically by author last name over hundreds of volumes. It is not as up-to-date as the database.

Credo Reference. Credo.

The *Academic Core* collection has over 650 titles, with an emphasis on subject-specific encyclopedias, dictionaries, atlases, and reference handbooks. Short videos, high-resolution art images, photographs, and maps are also featured. All subject areas are covered, including literature, film, and the performing arts.

Dictionary of Literary Biography (*DLB*). Gale/Cengage, 1978–. Print and online.

This series provides both biographical and historical background on thousands of authors—and essayists, literary critics, historians, journalists, and biographers—as well as original essays of literary criticism. Each volume of the more than four hundred volumes of the print version focuses on an author or group of authors. The online version contains over 16,000 entries, including thousands of images, and allows you to search by keyword and author name.

Felluga, Dino Franco, editor. *The Encyclopedia of Victorian Literature.* Wiley Blackwell, 2015. Print and online.

The most comprehensive reference work available on Victorian literature and critical trends in Victorian scholarship. It contains more than 330 cross-referenced entries from top Victorian scholars around the world. The alphabetical format makes it easy to locate topics of interest. Bibliographies of suggested readings accompany each entry.

Gale Cengage Literary Criticism series. Gale/Cengage. Print.

Among the titles are *Twentieth Century Literary Criticism*, *Nineteenth Century Literary Criticism*, and *Contemporary Literary Criticism*. These large print sets are organized into historical periods and have entries for the authors who lived then. Each entry gives a compendium of literary criticism about the author's works (excerpts of articles and essays in the early volumes, full articles in later volumes) and biographical information about the author. Most of the content in these series is available online through Gale's *Literature Resource Center.*

Literary Criticism Collection (ipl.org/div/litcrit/)

A curated collection of Web sites with critical and biographical information about authors and their literary works. No longer being updated, it does not contain information about authors today. You can browse the list of sites by author, title of work, nationality of author, or literary period. In each author entry are links to several sites, biographical and otherwise.

Literary Reference Center. EBSCO.

Provides biographical information for more than 250,000 authors and contains overviews of literary works, essays of literary criticism, and book reviews. The authors covered span literary disciplines and historical periods.

Literary Resources on the Net (andromeda.rutgers.edu/~jlynch/Lit/)

A free directory of Web sites with information about English and American authors, literature, and literary criticism.

Luminarium: Anthology of English Literature (www.luminarium.org/)

> With material taken from *The Norton Anthology of English Literature*, *The Encyclopædia Britannica*, and *The Cambridge Guide to Literature in English*, among others, the site is organized by literary period but can also be navigated by clicking on a name in the list of authors near the bottom of the page. The entry for each author contains a list of works, a biography, criticism, and quotations.

Mitchell, Sally. *Daily Life in Victorian England*. Greenwood Press, 2009. Print.

> Provides information about the physical, social, economic, and legal aspects of daily life in Victorian England, with more than sixty illustrations and excerpts from primary sources. Deals with questions concerning laws, money, social class, values, morality, and private life.

Mitchell, Sally. *Victorian Britain: An Encyclopedia*. Garland, 1988. Print.

> An encyclopedia covering all aspects of the cultural, political, social, religious, and literary world of Victorian England.

Oxford Companions series. Oxford UP. Print and online.

> The volumes in this series are essentially encyclopedias for specific literary periods, movements, and genres. The entries are short and basic and cover individual authors as well as major publications and literary terms relevant to the time or topic. Many of the titles in this series are available through *Oxford Reference Online*.

Oxford Dictionary of National Biography. Oxford UP, 2004. Print and online.

> The online database has information on over 60,000 people, including authors, poets, dramatists, and film makers. Its goal is to be the national record of people who shaped British history and culture from the time of the Romans to the present. Indicates where each author's archival and manuscript collections are located.

Oxford Reference Online. Oxford UP.

> Provides access to information across Oxford University Press's vast collection of historical dictionaries, literary companions, and encyclopedias, in twenty-five subject areas, including literature, media

studies, and performing arts. The entries range from short, general overviews to in-depth essays.

Parini, Jay, editor. *Oxford Encyclopedia of American Literature*. Oxford UP, 2004. Print.

A four-volume encyclopedia with biographical entries for a wide variety of American authors, from Gwendolyn Brooks to Leslie Marmon Silko to James Baldwin. Each essay gives an overview of the author's life and works, and a "Further Reading" section gives scholarly sources of literary criticism. There are also entries on works of literature, literary movements, and genres, such as "The Beat Movement," "Detective Fiction," and "Vietnam in Poetry and Prose." An online version is available through *Oxford Reference Online*.

Perspectives in American Literature (www.paulreuben.website)

Provides biographical information on American authors, lists of works of literary criticism, and bibliographies. The author entries can be navigated by time period (e.g., "Early American Lit 1700–1800," "The Harlem Renaissance") or alphabetically by author. Some entries are simply links to other sites and a bibliography of works; others contain extensive biographies, chronologies, lists of awards, as well as bibliographies and links to outside sources.

Poetry and Short Story Reference Center. EBSCO.

Useful for finding full-text poems and short stories, but it also contains biographical information about poets and short story writers that are lesser known.

Scott-Kilvert, Ian. *British Writers*. Scribner, 1979–84. Print.

A collection of essays in seven volumes on writers who have made "significant contributions to British, Irish, and Commonwealth literature." The writers are from the fourteenth century to 1979 but are limited to the traditional literary canon, so there are few essays on women authors or writers of color.

Voices from the Gaps (hdl.handle.net/11299/164018). American Periodicals Series.

A Web site designed to "uncover, highlight, and share the works of marginalized artists, predominately women writers of color living and working in North America." Now archived, it can be searched by author, title of her work, time period, or ethnicity. You can also browse by subject or category. Author entries include a biography and bibliography.

Wynne-Davies, Marion. *Bloomsbury Guide to English Literature*. Bloomsbury, 1989. Print.

Helpful in giving you a sense of literary periods and movements in their historical and social contexts. The bulk of this resource is made up of a reference section structured like a dictionary of English literature: short entries for authors and other literary figures as well as items, terms, and topics that have anything to do with English literature. There is also an essay section with titles such as "Political History and Social Context" and "Culture and Consciousness: The Twentieth-Century Novel."

Other

Chicago Manual of Style. 17th ed., U of Chicago P, 2017.

A comprehensive manual for authors, editors, proofreaders, and others involved in the publishing world. This edition contains new sections in response to developments in technology and source materials.

Harner, James L. *Literary Research Guide: An Annotated Listing of Reference Sources in English Literary Studies*. Modern Language Association of America, 2008. Print.

Documents all the major research tools and resources available for the study of literature: specialized dictionaries and encyclopedias, bibliographies, guides to manuscripts and archival collections, guides to primary works, guides to finding scholarship and criticism, guides to finding dissertations and theses, biographical sources, periodicals, and tools for finding resources by genre. A valuable resource for the literature scholar and student.

Johns Hopkins Guide to Literary Theory and Criticism. 2nd ed., Johns Hopkins UP, 2005. Print and online.

> The goal of this guide is to serve as a comprehensive historical survey of both ideas and individuals, from Plato to key twentieth-century scholars. Its entries are on critics and theorists, critical schools and movements, and the critical and theoretical innovations of different countries and historical periods.

Knowles, Elizabeth, editor. *Oxford Dictionary of Quotations*. 7th revised ed., Oxford UP, 2009. Print and online.

> Not all of the more than 20,000 quotations in this dictionary, which are fully indexed, pertain to literature, but this is one of the more thorough resources for covering literary works and writers. The online edition is available as part of the *Oxford Reference Online*.

Literary Research: Strategies and Sources series. Scarecrow Press, 2005–. Print and online.

> This series recommends the best tools for conducting specialized period and national literary research. Volumes emphasize research methodology and address the challenges presented by each literary period. Covered are general literary reference materials, library catalogs, bibliographies, scholarly journals, contemporary reviews, period journals and newspapers, microform and digital collections, manuscripts and archives, and Web resources.

MLA Handbook. 8th ed., Modern Language Association, 2016. Print and online.

> The authority on research and writing for students and scholars of literature. It explains how to evaluate sources, how to cite them, and how to create entries for works-cited lists.

Oxford English Dictionary (OED). 2nd ed., 20 vols., Clarendon–Oxford UP, 1989. Print and online.

> The authority on the English language. Provides not only definitions of words but also provides information on their origin, history, and pronunciation. When you read English authors from earlier time periods, having access to the *OED* is critical for understanding the use of certain words.

Princeton Encyclopedia of Poetry and Poetics. 4th ed., Princeton UP, 2012. Print and online.

> This encyclopedia is the most comprehensive and authoritative resource on aspects of poetry: history, movements, genres, prosody, rhetorical devices, critical terms, and more. Over a thousand entries give the *Encyclopedia of Poetry and Poetics* its unparalleled breadth and depth on the subject of poetry.

Publication Manual of the American Psychological Association. 6th ed., APA, 2010.

> A style manual designed for writers, editors, students, and educators in the social sciences disciplines. Provides guidance on grammar, the mechanics of writing, and using the APA style. It gives guidelines and examples for referencing electronic and online sources.

Purdue OWL. Purdue U.

> The Online Writing Lab (OWL) at Purdue University collects writing resources and other instructional materials for students who need help with grammar, citation style, and other aspects of their assignment. Under the category "Writing about Literature" are resources on literary terms, literary theory, and schools of criticism.

Glossary

academic discipline. A branch of knowledge that is studied by students and researched by faculty members in higher education (e.g., literature and languages, history, biology, political science). Generally thought of as broader than an academic field, which is a scholar's area of expertise in the discipline.

analyze. To break down a work of literature into distinct pieces or parts (e.g., themes, symbols, motifs, characters) and study them so as to better understand the whole.

annotation. A brief summary describing the subject or thesis of an article, book chapter, etc.

appendix. Usually located in the back, an appendix supplies additional or supplementary information about the topic covered in the main portion of the work. A book or an essay could have an appendix.

authority. The standing, credibility, or expertise that a person or organization has on a particular subject. Often denoted by certain education or training credentials or by work and life experiences.

bibliographic record. An entry in a library database or catalog that provides basic information about the item, such as author, title, and publication date.

bibliography. A list of all of the sources used (books, journals, Web sites, periodicals, etc.) in the process of researching and writing a paper. The list has different names, depending on its function and the citation style you are using (e.g., *works cited* in MLA style, *references* in APA style).

Boolean operators. Words (AND, OR, NOT) that are used to connect terms in various ways to determine how a database, search engine, or library catalog searches for the terms. They can expand or narrow a search or make sure that certain terms do not appear in search results.

citation chaining. Using the bibliography of a book or article to find more sources for your research.

citation style. A citation is a reference to a book, article, or author that you are quoting, paraphrasing, or summarizing, or it can simply tell readers where you got your idea. A citation style is a set of rules for formatting and presenting documentation elements.

confirmation bias. A psychological response to new information in which you are more likely to believe something that confirms what you already think to be true and less likely to believe something that goes against it. In research, where the goal is to learn new things based on new evidence, this tendency should be acknowledged and resisted.

consortium. A group of libraries, often in the same geographic region, that has an agreement to share materials and in other ways work as a single entity (e.g., with database vendors).

contemporary. Something that happened or was produced in or just before or after an author's lifetime, like diaries, letters, and book reviews. Something described as contemporary in the present means it happened or was produced during our lives.

credentials. Aspects of a person's background that indicate the person is qualified to write about a specific subject—a degree, a publication history, awards.

database. Large collection of data organized especially for rapid search and retrieval by a computer. Your library discovery system or catalog is a type of database—the data it organizes are information about books, articles, DVDs, maps, and so on.

debatable. A topic for which there are good, reasonable arguments that could be made on both (or several) sides. Obvious truths, facts, and plot points are not debatable.

discovery system (catalog). The system where you can find scholarly and popular books, scholarly journal articles, popular magazine and newspaper articles, government documents, maps, movies, music, and anything else that your library might physically own or have electronic access to.

dissertation. A long critical essay on a subject, especially one written as a requirement for the PhD degree.

facets, limiters. In a database, library discovery system, or library catalog, these are the options that allow you to home in on what you are looking for, to narrow search results by type of resource, date, subject, author, and so on.

fields (searching). When searching a library database, you can specify where to search for a certain word in the record. For instance, you can search for a particular author of an article or search for a specific publication date by limiting to the "Author Field" or "Date Field."

index. An alphabetical list of names, subjects, and topics covered in a book. Each item includes a reference to the places in the text where they occur. The index is almost always found at the end of a book.

interlibrary loan. A service that allows a patron of one library to borrow books, DVDs, or copies of articles that are owned by another library.

in-text citation. How you note in the text of your paper the instances in which you are summarizing, paraphrasing, or quoting another person's words or ideas in your writing. The formatting of in-text citations varies according to the citation style you are using.

iterative. A process that repeats is iterative. Good research is not a smooth, linear process but involves many iterations: the researcher repeats a series of steps as information is gathered, topics of interest are discovered, and new things are learned.

keywords. The words used to search for sources, usually on the Internet or in library databases, during the research process.

Library of Congress subject headings. An index of standardized terms or vocabulary created and maintained by the United States Library of Congress. Every published book is assigned a set of subject headings that describe what it is about.

literary criticism. The analysis or interpretation of a piece of literature, often with the support of secondary sources, to explain, illuminate, or recontextualize it.

open access. Scholarship that is openly available online, free of cost or other barriers for use. Often coupled with a Creative Commons license that gives people the right to use the scholarship fully in the digital environment.

open source. Code for a computer program that is freely available and modifiable by users and that therefore is continuously updated, changed, and improved by many developers.

paraphrase. To restate someone else's text in your own words, generally instead of using a direct quotation, to achieve clarity and consistency in your paper. If no reference is given for the paraphrase, even though it is not a quotation, you are plagiarizing.

peer review. The review of a scholar's book or article by a group of other scholars in the same academic field. The group evaluates the work and the contribution that it makes to their field and says whether or not it should be published.

periodical. A magazine, journal, or newspaper that is published at regular intervals. These intervals can be daily, as many newspapers are, monthly, or, as some scholarly journals are, annual.

persuasive. A paper is persuasive if it takes a position on a certain topic or issue related to the literary work being studied and attempts to convince the reader of the superiority of a certain interpretation, judgment, or conclusion.

plagiarism. Using other people's words or ideas without attribution, intentionally or unintentionally passing them off as one's own.

popular magazine. Publications that are written and intended for a general audience. Examples are *Newsweek, Atlantic Monthly*, and *People*.

primary sources. In literature, these artifacts typically fall into two categories: the creative work itself, both in published and manuscript form; or a work that was written or published during the author's lifetime.

reference source. A work that provides general, easily accessible, and digestible information about a topic. It could include a bibliography or a list of further reading for a more in-depth treatment of the topic. Examples are encyclopedias, biographical and historical dictionaries, handbooks, indexes, and concordances.

research guides. Online guides created by librarians that give information and advice on researching particular subjects. They contain many databases, library resources, and Web sites as well as guidance on conducting research and using the information you find in your research assignment.

scholarly journals and books. The peer-reviewed publications in which scholars publish the results of their work for other scholars.

scope. In a scholarly journal or for an academic publisher, *scope* refers to the type of work that it publishes, whether or not the work is peer-reviewed work, and how much of a subject matter or area it covers.

search algorithm. The coding created by computer programmers that Internet search engines and library databases use to retrieve information. It produces results based on search terms entered by the user and on various other factors.

secondary sources. Works that discuss, analyze, critique, interpret, debate, or otherwise engage with primary sources.

summarize. To condense the main idea of a work into a brief sentence or paragraph. If no reference is given for the summary, even though it is not a direct quotation, you are plagiarizing.

trade publication. A publication whose target audience is people working in a particular trade or industry. For example, *Publisher's Weekly* focuses on information of interest to those working in the book publishing or bookselling industry.

truncation. A searching technique in which an asterisk stands in for any combination of letters that follow. For example, *child** to find "children," "childhood," "childish," and "childlike."